AF591445

DISSERTATIO SECUNDA

De Jure quod competit

SOCIETATI PRIVILEGIATÆ FOEDERATI BELGII

Ad Navigationem & Commercia *Indiarum Orientalium*;

ADVERSUS

Incolas BELGII HISPANICI, hodie dicti, AUSTRIACI.

Qua respondetur objectionibus Viri Nobilissimi P. MAC. NENY, Sac. Cæs. & Cath. Suæ Majestatis Consiliarii & Procuratoris Fisci.

Mandatu DD. Directorum Societatis Privilegiatæ Indiarum Orientalium Fœderati Belgii conscripta ab ABRAHAMO WESTERVEEN Icto. eidem Societati a Consiliis & Secretis.

Ex Latina Anglicam fecit, & notis quibusdam auxit T. J.

HAGÆ COMITUM,
Apud THOMAM JOHNSON.
M. DCC. XXIV.

(2)

(2)

A SECOND DISSERTATION

Concerning the Right of the

DUTCH EAST-INDIA COMPANY

To the Trade and Navigation of the *East-Indies*,

AGAINST

The Inhabitants of the SPANISH, now AUSTRIAN, NETHERLANDS.

In anſwer to the objections of Mr. P. MAC NENY, Counſeor & Proc. Fiſcal, to His Imperial & Catholick Majeſty.

Written by order of the Directors of the Dutch Eaſt-India Company, *by ABRAHAM WESTERVEEN, Advocat, Counſellor & Secretary to the ſaid Company.*

Done into English, with ſome notes, by T. J.

HAGUE;
Printed for T. JOHNSON.
M. DCC. XXIV.

DISSERTATIO
SECUNDA,

De Jure quod competit SOCIETATI PRIVILEGIATÆ FOEDERATI BELGII,

Ad Navigationem & Commercia Indiarum Orientalium.

ADVERSUS

Incolas BELGII HISPANICI, hodie dicti AUSTRIACI.

A SECOND
DISSERTATION,

To prove the Right of the

DUTCH EAST-INDIA COMPANY,

AGAINST

The Inhabitants of the SPANISH, now AUSTRIAN NETHERLANDS.

Ostquam Hispaniarum Rex Art. IV. Fœderis Induciarum Anno 1609. septem Fœderatis Provinciis Navigationem & Commercia exercere ultra Europæ limites, ad Indiarum loca libera concesserat, ista conditione, ut a locis Hispanorum abstinerent, manentibus reliquis Belgii Provinciis sub prohibitionis Hispanicæ lege, ne ultra Europæ limites nagivarent; verum quidem est, (prout refert Solorzanus de jure Indiar. Lib. 2. Cap. 25.) Regem, quam primum tempus Induciarum exierat, bellum resuscitasse, quo tandem Batavos ab hujus Navigations & Commercis exercitio penitus abstinere cogeret. Verum hoc non ita ex sententia ipsi successit: contra enim anno 1648. pace facta evenit, ut Batavi sibi liberum stipulati sint, & obtinuerint totum illum tractum Maris, qui Privilegio a P. P. D. D. Ordinibus Societati Indiarum Orientalium antehac concesso, & a Rege deinceps agnito continebatur, cum exclusione subditorum Regis, ne ad limites fœdere prohibitos navigarent, aut navigationes suas ulterius extenderent, quam navigare ipsi tunc temporis erant soliti: sicut hoc ex sæpius allegato Articulo V. ejusdem fœderis jam ante probavimus, & nunc cum solutione eorum, quæ Belgii Hispanici, hodie Austriaci Incolis, contra verum hujus Articuli sensum objicere placuit, paulo amplius sumus probaturi.

I. Quod ut eo compendiosius peragatur, putamus totam hanc quæstionem, ad hæc tria capita commode reduci posse: & Primo quidem, quod Prædicti incolæ urgere conantur, sub lege prohibitionis dicti Art. V. Pacis Monast. solummodo comprehendi Castellanos, seu Hispanos, at non reliquos, qui tempore illius fœderis Regi Hispaniarum erant subjecti, veluti Brabantos & Flandros.

Secundo, Ne ipsos quidem Castellanos, sive Hispanos, eodem articulo a toto tractu maris, quo ante Fœdus Monasteriense navigare non erant assueti, exclusos fuisse; sed tantum à singulis locis Societati Fœderati Belgii in hoc tractu propriis, reliquum vero mare ipsis atque omnibus liberum mansisse voluit.

Tertio, Si forte concedant isto Prohibitionis pacto, Belgii Hispaniarum Incolas æque ac Hispanos teneri, contendunt tamen illud ad Imperatorem Romanum minime pertinere, qui Belgicas Provincias, ut ajunt, non acquisivit, nec possidet tanquam successor Philippi IV. Hispaniarum Regis, qui Fœdus Monast. cum Fœderato Belgio fecit; aut tanquam hæres Caroli II. postremo defuncti Regis, sed tanquam Burgundiæ Dux; non secus, ac Duces Burgundiæ easdem Provincias possederunt, antequam in ditionem Regum Hispano-

rum

BY the IV. Article of the Truce concluded in 1609. the King of Spain allowed the Inhabitants of the united Provinces to carry on their Trade & Navigation, without the bounds of Europe, to all free places of the Indies; with this restriction only, that they should not go to such places as were in the possession of the Spaniards: Whereas the Inhabitants of the other Provinces, or Spanish Netherlands, remained still under the restraint of the Spanish prohibition, by which they were forbid to navigate beyond the limits of Europe. 'Tis true, as *Solorzanus* says, that the King of Spain, as soon as the Truce was expired, began the war again that he might oblige the Dutch entirely to abstain from that Trade & Navigation. But he did not succeed in that according to his intentions: on the contrary, by the Treaty of Peace made in 1648. the Dutch stipulated & obtained that whole extent of seas comprehended in the Patent that the States had granted to their East-India Company, which was afterwards allowed by that King, while his own Subjects were excluded, from navigating to such places as were prohibited by the Treaty, & forbid to extend their navigation beyond what they were then accustomed to doe. This has been already proved by the V. Article of the Treaty of 1648. & shall be here further illustrated, with answers to such objections as have been made on behalf of the inhabitants of the Spanish, now Austrian Netherlands, against the true intention of that Article.

De Jure Indiar. L. II. C. 23.

To do this with more clearness & brevity, we shall divide this whole dispute into these three heads, which comprehend all the Arguments offered in favour of the present Inhabitants of the Austrian Netherlands.

I. They pretend that the Prohibition contained in the said V. Article of the Treaty of Munster concerns only the Castillans or Spaniards, but not any other people then subject to the K. of Spain, such as those of Flanders & Brabant.

II. That even the Castillans or Spaniards themselves, are not excluded by the said Article from the whole extent of sea which they did not use to navigate before the Treaty of Munster, but only from such places in those seas as were then possess'd by the Dutch E. India Company, so that all other places of those seas remained free & open for them & all others.

III. That supposing this Prohibition in the V. Article aforesaid should concern the Inhabitants of the Spanish Netherlands, as well as the Spaniards themselves; yet that does not concern his present Imp. Majesty, who has not (as they say) acquired, or does not possess those Netherlands in quality as Successor to Philip IV. K. of Spain, who made that Treaty with the Dutch, nor yet as Heir to K. Charles II. last deceased; but as Duke of Burgundy, with the same rights & prerogatives as they were possessed by the Dukes of Burgundy be-

rum transiissent, hoc est, purè & ab hac pacto seu Prohibitionis lege immunes, quales illas ante ætatem, Philippi I. cognomento Pulcri fuisse volunt.

CAP. I.

§. I. Quod attinet ad primam quæstionem, diximus antea incolas Belgii Hisp. a tempore detecti novi Orbis, usque dum prædicta Provinciæ in ditionem Cæsareæ suæ Majestatis redacta sunt, ad commercia Indiarum sive Orientalium, sive Occidentalium, nunquam admissos, sed expressis legibus inde prohibitos fuisse; & probavimus illud non solum antiquis Hispan. legibus, *quæ omnes alienigenas, præter Hispanos, ab his Commerciis excludunt; sed etiam per* Instrumentum Cessionis, *quo Belgii Provinciæ, a Philippo II. Archiducibus Alberto & Isabellæ ceduntur, hac expressa conditione adjecta,* ne unquam ad Indias Orientales seu Occidentales, Commerciorum causa Navigationem instituerent. *Probavimus præterea per* Articulum 4. Fœderis Induciarum, *quo solis Unitis Provinciis facultas data est commercia exercendi ultra Europæ limites ad ea loca, quæ in dissitis Indiarum regionibus essent sui juris, & libera; Reliquis vero Decem Provinciis, Archiducibus subjectis, eadem libertas minime indulta est, utpote quæ generalibus & expressis dicti Articuli verbis intra Europæ limites coërcentur. Probavimus hoc etiam, sed obiter, per id quod contigit Antverpiæ, secundum relationem* Em. a Meteren, *Anno* 1600. *& tandem etiam per constantem usum, & continuam harum legum ac Fœderis Monasteriensis observantiam, ad hanc usque ætatem.*

Atque hæc certa esse, nec cuiquam dubia videri posse putassemus, nisi vir Nobiliss. D. P. Mac Neny, auctor libri, cui titulus: Refutation des argumens avancés de la part de Messieurs les Directeurs des Compagnies d'Orient & d'Occident des Provinces-Unies, contre la liberté du commerce des habitans des Païs-Bas, &c. *nuper Bruxellis editi, dum partem seu Societatem commerciorum nostrorum ad Indiarum oras, Belgii Hispanici, hodie Austriaci Incolis vindicare studuit, omnia iret inficias; quamquam ipse passim tam obscure & implicite loquitur, ut plerisque in locis magis intelligi possit, quid omnino non dicat vel probet, quam quid dicere, aut ex dictis concludere velit. Sic, cum probare nititur §. 7.* Refutationis suæ, *legem de prohibita Navigatione ad Indias in Brabantia semper visam esse injustam, allegat quidem locum ex dicto à* Meteren Lib. 20. *ubi reperitur epistola incerti autoris, qui plurima referens de iniquitate dicti* Instrumenti Cessionis, *inter alia iniquum esse ait, Belgii incolas ab Indicis commerciis in æternum exclusos esse; sed nihil inde elicit aut concludit: Præterea, sicut hæc epistola publico nomine scripta non est, & ne in ipsa quidem Brabantia, ut videtur, sed alibi a quodam anonymo, quamvis ad Prælatum quendam in Brabantiam missa sit, ex*

eodem

fore they fell under the dominion of Spain; that is independent & free from any such restraint or convention, so as they were, say they, before Philip the first, Duke of Burgundy.

S E C T. I.

As to the first head, we have already said that the Inhabitants of the Spanish Netherlands, ever since the discovery of the new world, to the time that those Provinces were brought under the dominion of his Imperial Majesty, have never been allowed to have any trade to the Indies either East or West; but that they have by express laws been restrained from it. And this we have proved, not only by the old Laws of Spain, which exclude all others beside Spaniards from any such trade, but also by the Act of Cession by which *Philip II.* yielded those Provinces to the Archduke & Dutchess *Albert* & *Isabel*, with this express restriction, *that they should never undertake any navigation on account of trade to either East or West-Indies.*

Another proof of this we took from the IV. Article of the Truce made in 1609. by which the United Provinces only are allowed to trade without the limits of Europe, to all free & independent places of the Indies: wheras no such liberty is granted to the other Ten Provinces under the Archduke; but they are restrained within the limits of Europe by the general express words of that Article. For a further proof we mentioned cursorily what happened at Antwerp in 1600. as it is related by *Em. van Meteren*: & to confirm all these proofs we shewed the continued practice & constant observation of those Laws & Treatys to this present time.

These proofs & reasons we imagined were so plain & clear as to leave no doubt with any reasonable man: yet we see them all controverted by Mr. Mac Neny a Gentleman at Brussels, in a piece lately printed there called *A Confutation of the Reasons alleged by the Directors of the East & West-India Companys of the United Provinces, against the liberty of trading to forreign Climats by the Inhabitants of the Netherlands subject to his Imp. Maiesty* &c. In which the Author endeavours to establish a certain right which he thinks should belong to the Inhabitants of those Austrian Netherlands to share with us in our Navigation & trading to the East & West-Indies: tho' he is so perplexed & intricate in all that piece, that it is much easier to perceive what he does not prove, than what he does or would prove from most of the reasons he adduces. As in the 7. Sect. of his *Confutation* &c. to prove that this restraining from all commerce to the Indies was always deemed unjust in Brabant, he quotes a place of the aforesaid *Van Meteren* where mention is made of a Letter written by, one knows not who, which taking notice of several unjust things in the *Act of Cession*, among the rest says, ,, it was not just that all the Inhabitants of the Low ,, Countrys should be for ever excluded from all concern in the Indies. But he neither proves any thing, nor draws any conclusion from this; nor indeed could he from a nameless Letter, owned by no body, nor, it seems, writen in Brabant,

eadem a Meteren lib. 20. in princ. fol. 431. *evidenter apparet, Brabantiæ Proceres cum juramentum fidelitatis super actu Cessionis præstandum esset, de hac re nihil conquestos esse, considerantes hæc ita Regibus & Principibus suis antiquitus visum esse, nec non Pontifici Maximo sic placuisse, seque illud interdictum commune habere cum cæteris Regis subditis, & quodammodo etiam cum aliis Europæ populis, qui Regis subditi non erant; unde etiam post Pacem Monasteriensem Antverpiensis Jctus Franciscus Zypæus in libro, cui titulus,* Notitia Juris Belgici, lib. 12. cap. ultimo *justitiam Regis prohibentis hæc commercia laudibus extollit, atque hæc memoriæ posteritatis mandare nullus dubitavit. Verba ejus sunt hæc :*

De navigatione Indica cæteris gentibus, præter Hispanos atque Lusitanos prohibita, atque ut mare non liberum, ut voluit Grotius, sed potius Iberum hodie est censendum, diximus in *Jure Pontificio Nov. Anal. titul. de Summa Trin.* in fine. Eamque navigationem Alexander VI. commerciorum aliave quacunq de causa susceptam prohibuit, sub excommunicationis latæ sententiæ pœna; merito ut præmium Insularum illis Regibus, qui tam sanctam operam fidei propagandæ navassent in iis detegendis, cederet non tantum, sed & ne rectæ fidei cunabula ibi contaminarentur ab iis, qui domi suæ religionem conspurcassent: qua de causa, pluribusque politicis, si recte Josaphat Rex Judæ noluit Regem Israel ad classem suam, in insulam Ophir ex more majorum navigantem, ad auri opumque societatem admittere. Rex Chatholicus, ne alii in Indias navigent tam juste armis prohibet, quam legibus interdicit.

§. II. *Sic etiam §. 7.* Refut. suæ, supradict. D. Neny *negat incolas Belgii Provinciarum, qui Archiducibus erant subjecti, per* art. 4. fœderis Induciarum *anni* 1609. *à commerciis Indiarum exclusos esse, vel potius, ut ante fuerant, exclusos mansisse, quod* Dissert. nostræ §. 4. & 5. *notaveram; non ut inde inferrem exclusionem seu prohibitionem illam respectu nostri esse obligatoriam, propterea quod* eodem articulo *incolis Fœderatarum Provinciarum libertas ad hæc commercia certis quibusdam conditionibus datur; sed unice ut demonstrarem, Fœderatas Provincias a prohibitione generali de non navigando ultra Europæ limites exemtos esse, adeoque hoc articulo libertatem illis esse datam, quæ cæteris Provinciis data non est: quod ut clarius liqueat, integrum d. art. textum ex versione Latina* D. Baudii, *aut alterius cujuscunque autoris, ut invenitur post tractatum prædicti* Baudii de Induciis pag. 308. *hic exhibebo.*

Subditi & Inquilini utriusque partis, tam Regis & Archiducis, quam Fœderatorum Ordinum, invicem colunto mutuam benevolentiam & amicitiam, nec fas jusque esto præteriti temporis damna vel offensiones ulcisci aut exprobare: *Sunto libera utriusque negociandi Commercia per terras, maria, per flumina, quod tamen*

bant, but in some other place, & pretended to be sent to a certain Prelat in Brabant. But another thing (which this Author has not thought fit to take any notice of) appears very plain from *Van Meteren*, that the States of Brabant when they swore allegiance to the Archduke, upon this Act of Cession, made no complaint on account of this Prohibition, nor any mention of it in their Remonstrance; seing this had been always so ordered by their Kings or Princes, was so decided by the Pope, & was common to them with many others of the Kings Subjects, & in some measure with other Nations of Europe which were not Subjects of that King. And we see that even after the Treaty of Munster, a famous Lawyer of Antwerp *Francis Zypeus* in his Book entitled, *The Knowledge of the Belgic Law*, extolls with high praises the Kings justice in forbiding this trade to the Indies, in these following words.

Lib. XX. fol. 411. See this Remonstr. consist. of 17. Articles *ibid.*

Lib. XII. Cap. ult.

,, Concerning the navigation to the Indies forbid to all other people beside the ,, Spaniards & Portugese, & how the seas are not now to be esteemed free, as ,, Grotius would have them, but rather entirely *Spanish*, I have treated, *in* ,, *Jure Pontif. nov. anal. Tit. de Sum. Trin. in fine.* This Navigation, whe- ,, ther undertaken on account of Trade, or on any other account whatsoever, is ,, also prohibited by Pope Alexander VI. on pain of Excommunication *ipso* ,, *facto*; not only that the benefit of those Islands might belong only to those ,, Kings that had so much contributed to the holy work of propagating the Gospel ,, in discovering them, but also that the true Religion might not be defiled there ,, in its infancy, by such as had polluted it in their own countrys: for which, & ,, many other political reasons, as *Jehosaphat*, King of Juda, justly refused to ad- ,, mit the King of Israel into Society in the fleets he sent, as his predecessors ,, had done, to *Ophir* to bring Gold & precious things, so the King of Spain, ,, with equal justice, restrains by Arms, & forbids by Laws all others from tra- ,, ding to the Indies.

§ II. Mr. *Neny* pretends that the Inhabitants of the Netherlands, Subjects of the Archduke & Durchess were not excluded from all commerce with the Indies by the IV. Art. of the Treaty of Truce in 1609. or did not continue as they had formerly been under such an exclusion or restriction, so as I had laid down in my former Dissertation; not with design to prove that that prohibition was obligatory with regard to us, because by that Article the liberty of trading to the Indies was allowed to the United Provinces on certain conditions; but only to shew that the United Provinces were exempted from the general prohibition of trading without the bounds of Europe, & so had obtained by that Article a liberty which was not granted to the other Provinces. To make this more plain we shall here set down the said Article as it stands in President *Jeannin*'s Negociations.

Refut. Sect. 7.

Sect. 4. & 5.

T. 2. p. 449.

,, The Subjects & Inhabitants of both sides, that is of the said King & ,, Archduke, & of the said States, shall live in good amity & friendship with one ,, another during this Truce, without resenting the losses or injuries they may

have

men Rex Hispaniarum cupit restringi ad Regiones, terras ac provincias, quas possidet in Europa, vel ad alia regna dominiaque, quò Regum aut Principum amicorum subditi negociandi causa commeare solent: ab iis vero locis, portubus atque insulis, quæ extra fines prædictos sub ejusdem Regis imperio sitæ sunt, Ordines eorumque subditi abstinento, neque eò commerciorum causa proficiscuntor, nisi impetrato Regis consensu commeatuque. *Quod vero attinet ad loca, quæ aliis Regibus,* ,, *Proceribus aut populis subjecta sunt, etiam extra limites Europæos, licet Ordinibus eorumque subditis iis in locis ac regionibus commercari ac negociari; dum id fiat, permittentibus locorum dominis.*,, nec ullam moram aut impedimentum objiciet Rex ejusque Ministri, Vicarii aut Officiarii, quo minus domini locorum eam libertatum suo arbritatu concedant; nec ipsis Ordinum subditis negotium aut molestiam facesset, quo minus eo jure commeandi commercandique libere utantur.

Videmus igitur hic duas res *agi*, & primo *quidem commercia omnium incolarum totius Belgii per mare, per terras & flumina, intra Europæ limites restringi, atque illis ne libertatem quidem concedi, ut navigare liceat ad Regiones Indiarum liberas:* deinde *hanc libertatem solis PP. DD. Ordinibus eorumque subditis dari, modo ista navigationis & commerciorum exercitio fiat cum permissione domini loci, & ab Hispanorum locis abstineant.*

§. III. Porro cum memoratus D. Neny eodem §. 7. *probare conatur, Belgii Hisp. incolas hisce Fœderibus & Edictis non paruisse, aut saltem ex capite prohibitionis ab Indiarum commerciis non abstinuisse; sed forsitan, ut ait, quia hæc commercia sibi haud utilia fore putabant; non allegat actus aliquot contrarios, quibus illos re vera non paruisse constet, aut contra hæc edicta prohibitoria nihilominus navigare solitos esse, sed negat apud* dictum à Meteren *reperiri historiam, qualis illa compendiose narratur in* Remonstratione D D. Directorum Societatis Indiarum Orientalium, *tradita PP. DD. Ordinibus mense Martio anni* 1720. *& quam brevitati studens contractiorem aliquantulum repetivi* Dissertat. nostra §. 2. *tempe*: cum initio præteriti seculi anno 1600. Mercatores quidam Antverpienses tentassent per ambages, sive nomine Batavorum Mercatorum, aut, ut ait dictus à Meteren, sub Hollandis pecunias suas impendere ad commercia Indica; Regem Hisp. hoc tam ægre tulisse, ut virum honoratum, nomine Gusman, Antverpiam ablegaverit ad perscrutandos mercatorum libros, & inquirendum, quis consors & particeps esset ejusmodi commerciorum, quæ à Rege erant prohibita; donec post multas persecutiones, quas ob hanc aliasque res illicitas erant perpessi, tandem Belgii incolæ illud gravi exactione 600000. ducatorum luere sunt coacti.

Sed

„ have suffered heretofore. They may also freely travel & sojurn in one anothers countrys, & safely trade or commerce with one another by land or water. Which according to the said Kings intentions should be restrained to the Kingdoms Countrys & Provinces that he is possessed of in Europe, or to such places & seas where the Subjects of other Kings or Princes his Friends & Allys have such trade with mutual consent of parties. But to such places Towns, ports or harbours as he is possessed of without the said limits, it shall not be lawful for the said States or their Subjects to trade in any sort, without express leave from the said King. Yet it shall be lawfull for them to trade, if they think fit, into the Countrys of any other Princes States or people that will allow them, even without those limits; and the said King or his Officers, Subjects, or dependants shall give no let or hinderance on that account to any such Princes States or People that shall give such allowance, nor yet to them, or others with whom they so trade.*

We see here two things plain in this Article: 1. that all the commerce of the Inhabitants of the whole Low Countries was confined within the bounds of Europe, & that it was not lawfull for any of them to navigate to any place of the Indies. 2. That this liberty was granted to the States of the United Provinces & their Subjects only, provided they were allowed by the Soverains of the places, & that they abstained from places possessed by the Spaniards.

III. WHEN Mr. *Neny* pretends to shew that the Inhabitants of the Spanish Netherlands never had any regard to those Laws or conventions, or that they never abstained from trading to the Indies on that account; but perhaps, says he, because they did not think that trade worth their pains; he does not produce any Acts or proofs to shew that they refused to obey those Laws, or that they attempted any such trade contrary to the Prohibition, but contents himself to affirm boldly that there is no such passage in *Van Meteren*'s History, as that which is mentioned in the Remonstrance of the Directors of our East-India Company to the States in March 1720. & which for brevity's sake I resumed in my former Dissertation, *Sect.* 2. in these words. „ When towards the beginning of the last age, in 1600. several Merchants of Antwerp began in a clandestine manner, or under the names of Dutch Merchants, or, as *Van Meteren* says, of Hollanders, to employ their stocks in trading to the Indies, the King of Spain took this so heinously, that he sent a person of note to Antwerp to search the Merchants books, & examine who had taken part or share in such trade, forbiden by his Majesty; till after a great many vexations on this & other accounts at last the Flemish Merchants were forced to buy it off with a summ of 600000 ducats.

B Now

* There is a further confirmation of this liberty of trade in a separate or secret Article of the same date with this Treaty, by which the K. of Spain confirms the liberty here allowed the Dutch of trading to all places where the Soverains or people should suffer them, not only within the limits mentioned here, but every where else; & that they may trade safely & securely, promises solemnly to give no hinderance by sea or land, to them or those they trade with, &c. See *Negociat. de Jeanin To.* 2. *p.* 457.

Sed quid iterum de veritate historiæ, & vero sensu illius textus judicandum sit, nunc unicuique liquere poterit, dum integer locus, quanquam prolixus & variis rebus Append. No. I. *refertus, prout antiquitus Gallice redditus est, infra * exhibebitur: unde apparebit, quàm parum verosimile sit, quod Antverpienses clam & Hollandorum nomine, sive* sub Hollandis, *ut verba Historici sequar, commercia ad Indias exercuissent; quod prohibitoriis Principum legibus obtemperare detrectassent, quum nunquam ullam navem ad Indias ipsi miserint: quod utilitatem hujus commercii non novissent, quum lucri faciendi gratiâ pecunias suas Hollandis, tunc temporis Regis hostibus, eò navigantibus commiserint. Sed maxime omnium admirandum videtur, quod huic argumentationi addit prædictus* Dominus Neny, *nullum populum in his, quæ sunt meræ facultatis, jus suum non utendo, seu negligendo, amittere, modo non neglexerit, vel mi non omiserit, ex capite prohibitionis, dum ait:* Et il est egalement constant, que si quelques Nations negligent le commerce de ces sortes de lieux, elles ne perdent pas pour cela la liberté d'y commercer, quand elles le trouveront convenit, par quelque laps de temps que ce puisse être; puisqu'on ne peut dire, qu'il leur auroit été defendu, mais parce qu'elles n'avoient cru, qu'il leur fut avantageux.

§. IV. Si argumentum hoc sumatur a Contrario, certum est D. Neny *hoc ipso ratiocinio statuere, quod si ex causa prohibitionis aliquis neglixerit, aut omiserit jure suo uti, illum eo ipso jus suum amittere; quod verum esse, & in usu maris spectatim locum habere, Jurisconsulti communiter statuunt; ut videre licet apud Germanum Ictum* Georg. Jacob. Leikherrum de Jure maritimo cap. 8. *ubi agens de præscriptione navigationis* pag. 74. sic loquitur

Navigatio est actus meræ facultatis, contra quem non currit præscriptio, nisi prohibitione interveniente; *Coler. Cons. I. n. 397.* & tali tempore mare præscribi posse, & illud possidere, qui jurisdictionem & imperium in eo exercet, defendit *Cepoll. D. S. R. Præd. cap. 26. n. 5. 6. & 9.* imo breviori tempore sc, 30. annorum præscriptione hoc determinat *Schurdio. ad §. 1. de R. D.* Kling ad d. §. 1. *Item apud Maulium in Thesauro theor. præct. ibique in tract. de Jure marit, tit. 5. n. 5.* Nam si quis, *inquit*, per aliquot annos in certa maris parte piscatus sit, aut nav gaverit, aliosque prohibuerit, sciente populo & non contradicente, tunc habet sibi quæsitum jus ex tacito populi consensu. *Et paulo post:* Licet enim ea, quæ jure gentium communia sunt, præscribi non possunt, tamen consuetudine acquiri possunt, & impræscriptibilia acquiruntur consuetudine.

Quum autem ex dictis nihil manifestius eluceat, nec quicquam clarius probari possit, quam quod Belgii Hisp. incolæ, unice propter prohibitionis causam, ab Indiarum commerciis abstinuerint; & ab omni tempore inde prohibiti fuerint, tam Ecclesiasticis, quam Secularibus Constitutionibus & Edictis, non solum à Principibus suis, sed etiam

post

Now as to the truth of this history, & the true meaning of that passage, we leave every one to judge for himself, having set down the whole passage at length, Apend. No. I. tho' somewhat prolix & treating of different matters, as it is in the French translation published in 1618. From which every one will be able to judge how unlikely it is that the Merchants of Antwerp would undertake the trade to the Indies clandestinely, & under the name or cover of the Hollanders, if they had been free to doe it openly themselves; that they refused to obey the prohibition of their Soveraigns, when they never sent one ship to the Indies: that they did not think this trade would turn to account, when desirous to share in the profits of it they trusted their stocks to the Hollanders who were then at open war with them. But the most curious of all is what Mr. *Neny* adds to conclude this reasoning, *viz.*, that no people can lose the right they have to a thing of that nature by meerly neglecting to use that right &c. But take here his own words. „ It is „ also certain that if any people forbear to trade to such places, they do not for „ that lose the right to undertake such trading when they have a mind to it, by any „ lapse of years whatsoever; for it cannot be said they forbore it because it „ was forbiden, but because they did not think it worth their pains.

IV. LET us turn the other side this argument, & we will see clearly that M. *Neny* grants, that if people forbear the use of any right because it is forbidden, they thereby actually lose that right: which is true, & especially as to the use of the sea, according to the common opinion of Lawyers. As one may see by *G. J. Leikher*, a German Lawyer, *de Jure maritimo Cap. 8. p. 74.* where treating of Prescription in matters of Navigation he says „ Navigation is an act perfectly „ free, against which there can be no prescription, except by a prohibition. „ *Caler. Cons. 1. n. 397.* and in such a time there may be prescription, & the sea „ may be in the possession of him that exercises empire & jurisdiction in it, according to *Capoll. D. S. R. Prad. Cap. 26. n. 5. 6. & 9.* and this time is determined to a short space, *viz.* 30. years by *Schnydw.* ad §. I. de R. D. *Kling* ad d. „ § I. as likewise by *Maulius in Thesauro theoret. pract. in Tract. de jure Marit. Tit. 5.* „ *n. 5.* For, says he, if any one for a number of years has fished or navigated in „ a certain place of the Sea, & has forbid others to do so, those others having „ consented without any difficulty or contradiction, that person has acquired a „ right by the tacit consent of those others. *And a little lower;* For tho' such things „ as are common by the law of nations are not lyable to prescription, yet they „ may be acquired by long use, & even things *unprescribable* are acquired by „ custom.

So nothing is clearer, from what has been said, nor can be more clearly made out, than that the people of the Spanish Netherlands forbore trading to the Indies because of the prohibition; and that they have always been forbid that trade, both by Ecclesiastical & civil Constitutions & Edicts, & have been hindered not

B 2 only

post Fœdus Monasteriense, à Societate Privilegiata Fœderati Belgii; quod exemplo Bastiani Brouwer, *qui in litteris Præsidis & Senatus Indici appellatur* Hispano-Brabantus §. 6. dissert. nost. *probavimus: videat itaque* D. Neny, *atque ipse judicet, quantopere illud argumentum faciat contra seipsum; &, si de præscriptione hic ageretur, quam manifeste Belgii Austriaci incolis obstaret negligentia, sive non usus, non dicam per tempus longissimum, sed ab omni tempore ad hanc usque ætatem, quoniam nunquam usi sunt, neque uti potuerunt, eo quod dicta prohibitio illis semper obstitit.*

§. V. Sed non agit Societas Fœderati Belgii jure summo, nec ex præscriptionis causa, nec ex ipsis prohibitoriis Principum legibus, jus suum metitur, nisi quatenus hæc longissimi temporis usu confirmata tandem Pace Monasteriensi in vim obligationis transierunt. Agit itaque ex pacto, agit ex Fœdere Pacis cum Belgii Hisp. quondam Principe facto, quod perpetuum est, nec pace cum Hispanis & Lusitanis, ac Fœderato Belgio facta evanuit, ut vult D. Neny §. 2 Resist. Vers. Mais comme tous: *sed adhuc viget atque subsistit, non solum cum Rege Hisp. sed etiam cum Cæsarea sua Majestate, quatenus C. & C S. M. tanquam hæres & successor postremo defuncti Belgii Principis Caroli II. illud ipsum fœdus Antverpiæ firmavit; quod infra, cum debita tamen erga Summum Principem reverentia, latius demonstrare conabimur.*

Interea quæstio huc iterum recidit, an scilicet Hispaniarum Rex una tantum qualitate, tanquam Hispaniæ Rex, *an etiam altera, nempe ut* Burgundiæ Dux *sive* Dux Brabantiæ & Comes Flandriæ *Fœdus Monasteriense fecerit? adeoque an Belgii Hisp. incolæ clausula finali* art. 5. *ejusdem Fœderis, quatenus illic agitur de prohibita navigationis extensione, una cum Hispanis comprehendantur, nec ne? Nos Regem eadem qualitate, qua bellum in Belgio gessit, pro omnibus suis subditis, hoc est non solum tanquam Hispaniarum Regem, sed etiam tanquam Burgundiæ Ducem, illud fœdus fecisse, adeoque Belgii Hispanici incolas, una cum Hispanis* dicto articulo 5. *comprehendisse, antea asseruimus; & hoc probavimus ex natura & circumstantiis rei in conventionem deductæ; quæ talis est, ut ab his omnibus præstari potuerit, & debuerit. Probavimus etiam ex denominatione a potiori parte, nempe* Hispanorum & Castellanorum, *quæ sequiorem partem comprehendit; probavimus ex constanti usque ad hæc tempora usu, ex Pacis instrumentis, ex Fœderis Proœmio, Legatorum mandato, & ratihabitionis actu; quæ omnia Rex fecit, non solum tanquam Hisp. Rex, sed etiam tanquam Burgundiæ Dux pro se, posteris, subditis & successoribus omnium Regnorum, Dominiorum & Ditionum suarum; quatenus inter illos aliqui esse possent, qui Fœderato Belgio effectum hujus Fœderis adimerent; dum noluit, ut unquam quicquam in contrarium attentaretur.* Vide actum ratihab. & art. 76. Pacis Monast. *Nam si Principes, qui diversa Regna*

&

only by their own Princes, but also, after the Treaty of Munster, by our Dutch East-India Company, as I have proved § 6. of my former *Dissertat.* by the Example of *Bastian Brower* called in the Letters of the President & Council of the Indies a *Spanish Brabander.* Mr. *Neny* may now see how much this argument makes against him; & if the question were to be decided by prescription, how the Inhabitants of the Austrian Netherlands must lose their cause, because of their abstaining from, or not using that trade, not only in a very long time, but in all times till this present; as indeed they never did or could do it being always restrained by the aforesaid prohibitions.

V. BUT the Dutch East-India Comp. does not insist on the rigour of the Law, nor found its right barely on prescriptions, or on the Prohibitions of Princes; but on such as have been submitted to & confirmed by a very long use, & at last have obtained the force of the strongest obligation by the Peace of Munster. They go upon a Covenant; on a Treaty of Peace made with the Soverain of the Spanish Netherlands, which is perpetual; & far from being extinct as Mr. *Neny* would have it, it is yet in full force, not only with the King of Spain, but also with the Emperour, insomuch as His Imp. & Cath. Majesty, as Heir & Successor to the last deceased Soverain of the Spanish Netherlands *Charles II.* renewed it by a new Treaty at Antwerp, as we shall, with due respect to his said Majesty, more fully prove hereafter.

But a question is made, whether the King of Spain made the Treaty of Munster, only in one quality as K. of Spain, or in another also as Duke of Burgundy & of Brabant & Earl of Flanders; and consequently if the inhabitants of the Spanish Netherlands be comprehended with the Spaniards in the last clause of the fifth Article of that Treaty about the prohibition of extending their Navigation. I have already asserted that that King made the aforesaid Treaty for all his Subjects, in the same quality that he made war in the Low Countrys, that is not as King of Spain only but also as Duke of Burgundy; & so comprehended those of the Spanish Netherlands as well as the Spaniards in the said V. Article. This I proved by the nature & circumstances of the thing agreed on, which is such as might & ought to be performed by all. I proved it also by the denomination taken from the greater part, viz *Spaniards* or *Castillians.* I proved it also by constant use to these times; by the Instrument of the Treaty, & by the preamble; by the Instructions of the Ambassadours, & by the Act of Ratification: In all which that King acted not only as King of Spain but also as Duke of Burgundy, for himself & posterity, for his Subjects & Successors in all his Kingdoms, Dominions & States, in so far as there might be any of them that might refuse the effect of this Treaty to the United Provinces; for he would hinder that any thing should ever happen contrary to this. (see the Act of Ratification, & the 76 Art. of the Treaty) For if Princes who have several Kingdoms & Dominions, made use of such deno-

 minations

& Dominia possident, tali locutione a potiori parte, *quæ frequens est, & in fœderibus sæpe occurrit, ad excludendos alios uterentur, in casibus, qui natura sua tales sunt, ut nisi id quod promissum est, ab omnibus, qui contra facere possent, æque præstetur, tota promissio atque conventio statim corruat & stipulanti inutilis fiat, variæ absurditates sequerentur, quas bonæ fidei Foederum adversari* Dissert. nostr. §. 13. *demonstravimus: atque illic etiam docuimus, in causis ejusmodi verborum obscuritatem veritati rei, de qua actum est, cedere oportere; ne alias ridicula fiat conventio. Nam si P.P. DD. Ordines expressis verbis stipulati essent*, ne Hispanis navigationem ad limites Privilegii nostri ulterius extendere liceret, quam tunc temporis navigare erant assueti, *& contra consensissent*, ut Brabantis aut aliis Regis subditis id novo exemplo facere liceret, *ridenda esset stipulatio; quoniam Brabanti, si ad hanc navigationem admittantur, plus nocere queant, quam Hispani. Quapropter necessario corruit ista distinctio, quam* D Neny *crebro facit inter ea, quæ Philippus IV. fecit tanquam Hispaniarum Rex, & ea quæ fecit, tanquam Burgundiæ Dux; quum certum sit illum eadem qualitate, qua Bellum gessit, etiam Foedus hoc fecisse; & Hispaniarum Reges non minori potestate Belgis, quam Hispanis præfuisse; modo nihil facerent, quod Privilegiis Belgarum adversaretur, quibus jus Navigationis & Commercii ad Indias nunquam annumeratum est.*

§. *VI. Si quis tamen subtili disputandi ratione præcise roget, quo nomine aut qualitate memorati Hispaniarum Reges, Belgii incolas, suos subditos à commerciis Indiarum prohibuerint? respondendum videtur, illos hoc fecisse tanquam Burgundiæ Duces, & Belgii Principes in gratiam Hispanorum. Nam quum Philippus II. Provincias Archiducibus cessit, certum est illum hoc fecisse tanquam Burgundiæ Ducem, & hac qualitate etiam legem actui Cessionis dixisse, ne commercia ad Indias exercerent.* Atqui, *inquit* D. Neny, Burgundiæ Duces non tam absolutam in Belgas potestatem habuerunt, ut illos Privilegiis suis, & libertate naturali, suisque legibus fundamentalibus orbare potuerint. Refut. suæ §. 1. *Sed pace Viri Clarissimi dixerim, jactat Privilegium & libertatem, quam nunquam habuerunt, & qua destituti erant, antequam Hispaniæ Regnum & Burgundiæ Ducatus ad unum Principem devenirent. Nam quis Regum Hisp. à Ferdinando V. sive Catholico, quo regnante Christophorus Columbus anno* 1492. *regiones Americanas detexit, usque ad Philippum IV. qui Fœdus Monasteriense fecit, illis unquam dedit Privilegium aut libertatem navigandi ad Indias? quæ sequenti anno* 1493. *quum lis orta esset de hac navigatione inter Hispanos & Lusitanos, Constitutione Alexandri VI. P. R. statim ita divisæ sunt, ut pars Orientalis cederet Lusitanis, pars Occidentalis Hispanis; neque his supra Promontorium Bonæ Spei Orientem versus navigare liceret. Quamobrem illos iter ab* Oc-

minations as are commonly taken from the greater part & frequently used in Treaties, to exclude others, in cases of such a nature that unless the promise be keept by all that might act contrary to it, the whole convention would come to nothing & be of no effect, there would follow several absurditys, which I have Sect. XIII. shown in my former Dissertation would be contrary to the sacred faith of Treatys. I also made out there that in such cases the obscurity of the terms must give way to the truth or nature of the things in question, otherwise the convention would be ridiculous & useless. For exemple, if the States, stipulating in express terms that the Spaniards should not extend their navigation further within the limits of our Privilege than what they were accustomed to doe at that time, had allowed that the Brabanders or others of the Kings Subjects might undertake such Navigations; this would be a ridiculous stipulation, for the Brabanders being admitted to this Navigation could do us much more prejudice than the Spaniards. Therefore that distinction must fall to the ground which Mr. *Neny* so often makes, between what Phillip IV. did as King of Spain, & what he did as Duke of Burgundy: for 'tis certain that he made the Treaty in the same quality that he waged war with us; & that the Kings of Spain were as much Soverains of the Spanish Netherlands as of Spain; especially if they did not violate the Privileges of the inhabitants, among which the Right of Navigation & trade to the Indies was never reckoned.

VI. But if any one for the sake of cavilling were to ask, in what right or quality the aforesaid Kings of Spain prohibited their Subjects in the Netherlands from trading to the Indies? it may be answered that they did it as Dukes of Burgundy, and Soverains of the Netherlands to favour the Spaniards. For when Philip II. yielded those provinces to the Archduke and Dutchess, 'tis certain he did it as Duke of Burgundy, and in the same Right made that restriction in the Act of cession, prohibiting their commerce to the Indies. But, says Mr. *Neny*, the Duke of Burgundy had not so absolute a power over the Netherlands, as to deprive the inhabitans of their priviledges, their natural liberty, and their fundamental Ref. § 11 laws. But with that Gentlemans leave I must say he boasts of a priviledge and liberty which they never had, and were destitute of, even before the Kingdom of Spain and the Dukedom of Burgundy were united under one Prince. For what King of Spain, from Ferdinand V. or Catholick, (in whose reign Chr. Columbus, anno 1492. discovered the American coasts) to Philip IV. who made the Treaty of Munster, ever gave them priviledge or liberty of trading to the Indies? which Indies, the following year 1493. (when the contest about the Commerce to those parts began betwixt the Spaniards and Portugese) were thus divided by a Constitution of Alexander VI. then Pope. The Eastern parts to the Portugese, and the Western to the Spaniards; these last being to sail no farther east than the Cape of good hope: for which reason they sought a passage from the west by the

streits

Occidente per Fretum Magellanicum affectasse, & utrumque Regem propria & Pontificis auctoritate nixum, exinde omnes Europæ populos, tam subditos sibi, quam non subditos (exceptis solis Lusitanis & Castellanis, qui in detegendo Novo Orbe præcipuam operam navarant) ab aditu Indiarum severis legibus prohibuisse alibi monuimus. Successit Ferdinando Philippus I. qui primus fuit Hisp. Rex & Belgii Princeps; huic Carolus V. illi Philippus II. qui anno 1598. *utraque qualitate, & tanquam Rex in gratiam Hispanorum, & tanquam Princeps Belgii, per notissimum* Cessionis Actum, *hac navigatione Belgis interdixit, quos sequutus est Philippus III. qui solis Fœderatis Provinciis anno* 1609. *per Fœdus Induciarum navigationem ad Indiarum loca libera concessit, manentibus reliquis Provinciis sub antiquis tam Hispaniarum, quam Belgii legibus, ne ad Indiarum Regiones commerciorum causa navigare ipsis liceret. Quid fecit igitur Philippus IV. quum anno* 1648. *Indias Orientales, quas Societas nostra jam tum occupaverat, nobis cessit, quo his incolis nocuit? aut quid ademit illis, quod Reges ante ipsum non ademerant? Privatio præsupponit habitum; at qui non habuit, privatus dici non potest. Non reddidit igitur memoratus Rex illos deterioris conditionis, quam antea fuerant: sicut ab altera parte etiam certum est, Serenissimum Angliæ Regem, & P P. D D. Ordines, per Foedus anni* 1701. *quod Magnam Confoederationem vocant, & per subsequentem Tractatum* de Barriere, *illos non melioris conditionis facere voluisse ad tam insigne detrimentum subditorum suorum. Sed urget Clarissimus Auctor, illud interdictum Hispan. Regum Belgii incolis tantum commune fuisse cum cæteris Europæ populis, nempe Anglis, Gallis & similibus. Quasi vero Reges, qui simul erant Belgii Principes, non plus imperii habuissent in Belgas suos subditos, quam in Anglos & Gallos ipsis non subditos, quos ipso quidem facto ab Indiis arcere, jure prohibere non poterant! Quo etiam pertinent illa, quæ Philippus II. moriens filio & Successori suo Philippo III. mandavit, apud* E. a Meteren *lib.* 20. *fol.* 418. *cum dixit* Quantum ad Commercia Indiarum Orientalium & Occidentalium attinet, in illis consistit robur Imperii Hispanici, quo refrenantur Itali. At Gallos & Anglos ab his Commerciis prohibere non poteris, quoniam nimis sunt potentes; habent etiam magnam copiam sociorum nauticorum. Oceanus spatiosus est; Mercatores illorum sunt divites, milites rapaces, & subditi nimium fideles. At Belgas ipse prohibui pro te &c.

§ *VII. Verum ut quæstionem hanc, quæ distinctionibus istiusmodi magis magisque intricata redditur, ad pauca redigamus, alterutrum necessario statuendum*

est

ftraits of Magellan; and these Princes relying on their own and the Popes authority, together (as we have already remarked) forbid by severe laws all access to the Indies, not only to their own Subjects, but even to all the People of Europe excepting only the Portugese and the Castilians, who had the principle share in the discovery of those new lands. Philip I. succeeded Ferdinand, and was the first King of Spain who was Prince of the Netherlands. Charles V. succeeded Philip, and was himself succeeded by Philip II. who anno 1598 in a double quality as King of Spain and Soverain of the Netherlands, made that famous Act of Cession wherin he excluded the inhabitants of the said Netherlands from all such Commerce and navigation. After him came Philip III. who by the Truce in 1609 granted to the United Provinces only the liberty of trading to all free parts of the Indies, the rest of the Provinces remaining still under the old laws as well of Spain as of the Netherlands, by which they were restrained from making any voyages on account of trade to the Indies. What injury then did Philip de to those of the Spanish Netherlands, when in 1648. he yielded to the Dutch all those place of the East-Indies which they were already in possession of, any such other places as they should at any time recover from the Portugese? What did he take away from them which the Kings before him had not already taken? The loss of priviledges presupposes the being of those priviledges, so that those who never had them, can never be said to have lost them. The aforesaid King then can not be said to have reduced them to a worse state than they were in before. On the other hand also 'tis certain that his British Majesty, and our States, by the Treaty made in 1701 called the Grand Allyance, and afterwards by the Barrier Treaty, would by no means endeavour to better their condition as to that point, with a very manifest detriment to their own Subjects. But our Author urges, that the prohibition of Spain excluded all the People of Europe, as the English French, &c. equally with those of the Netherlands: As if the Kings of Spain, who were at the same time Soverains of the Netherlands, had had no more right to impose a prohibition on the inhabitants of those Netherlands who were their Subjects, than they had to impose the same on the English or French who were not so, & whom they might drive away by main force, but could not exclude them by any Law. To this purpose Philip II. when he was dying said to Philip III. his Successor---,, 'Tis in the Trade of the East and West-Indies that ,, the chief strength of the Spanish Monarchy consists, & the means of keeping Italy in subjection. You will not be able to exclude the French & English from that trade because they are too powerfull, and their naval ,, forces too great: The Ocean is wide, their Merchants are rich, their ,, Soldiers bold, and their Subjects loyal. But as for the Netherlanders I have ,, taken care to prohibit them for you &c. E. a Meteren lib. 10. fol. 418.

§ VII. But to bring into a narrow compass this question, which by distinctions

 of

est, nempe, aut verum esse, quod vult D. Neny *Belgii Hispanici incolas semper æquum jus cum Hispanis ad commercia Indiarum, tam Orientalium, quam Occidentialium, habuisse; aut non habuisse: medium enim non datur. Si statuamus illos cum Hispanis æquum jus semper habuisse; sequitur etiam eos clausula finali* d. art. 5. *una cum Hispanis inclusos esse; ne scilicet navigationes ad limites probibitos extenderent: si ponamus illos non habuisse, quod verissimum quidem est; bona fides Foederis tunc omnino exigit, ut ratione horum subditorum, cum Rege actum & contractum sit, quà talium; utpote quibus nullum jus ad commercia Indiarum competebat, propter leges & probibitiones illis tunc temporis obstantes; ne alias, salvis articuli verbis, mens ejus & sententia circumveniatur. Ut si, verbi gratia, Brabanti ab Ordinibus Foederati Belgii stipulati essent, ne Zeelandi prope limites Brabantinos piscarentur, & PP. DD. Ordines, hac promissione data, mox per Hollandos contra stipulationis istius intentionem id fieri sinant; aut, quod in pacto ultro citroque obligatorio nequaquam procedit, ut scilicet incolæ Foederati Belgii exclusi essent a toto tractu occiduo & Insulis Hispanorum in India Orientali sitis; contra, vero quodcunque Hispan. Rex nobis cessisset, non alia conditione cessum esset, quam ut illud, quandocunque ipsi commodum esset, iterum eripere & sibi vindicare posset; non quidem per Hispanos, sed per alios suos subditos, nobis quanto viciniores, eò magis nocituros, tam in Indiis, quam in hisce Europæ Regionibus. Certe si hoc modo contrahendum fuisset, aut PP. DD. Ordines unquam divinare potuissent, affuturum aliquando tempus, quo subtili disputandi ratione ad hanc iniquitatem deveniretur; scilicet distinguendo inter qualitates Principis, & utriusque contrahentis subditos, ut tam insigne caput Foederis Monasteriensis ipsis inutile fieret; præsumendum non est, eos tam subdola conditione pacem inituros; aut ineunte hoc seculo consensuros fuisse in Confoederationem Magnam, ut Belgii Provincias Cæsareæ suæ Majestati restituerent, sibique ipsis internecivum damnum hoc modo pararent. Quapropter & causam nostram meliorem esse nemo negabit; utpote qui agimus de damno vitando; qui rogamus, ne officium nobis damnosum sit; quàm illorum, qui certant de lucro captando: qui hic agimus de retinenda possessione, quam illi novo exemplo turbant, dum Commerciorum nostrorum societatem sibi impertiri & communicari postulant, etsi ad stabilienda hæc commercia ne hilum quidem contribuerint.*

§. VIII. *Sed, inquit* D. Neny §. 4. Refut. non ipse Hispaniarum Rex Carolus II. postremo defunctus, hæc ita intellexit. *At nos contra non tantum Hispaniarum Regem, sed & Cæsaream suam Majestatem ante annos aliquot hæc ita intellexisse videri (cum debita observantia) alibi diximus: & quantum ad Hispaniarum Regem pertinet, illud probavimus per constantem usum usque ad hæc tem-*

of this kind only becomes more and more intricate, one of these two things [for there is no medium] is necessarily true; either the inhabitants of the Netherlands, as Mr. *Neny* would have it, had always an equal right with the Spaniards of trading to the Indies: or they had not. If we say they had, it follows that they must be included with the Spaniards in the final clause of the V. Article, which forbids their trading beyond certain limits. If we say they had not, which is the truth of the matter, then the sacred faith necessary to Treatys requires that in contracting with the Soverain we must be supposed to have contracted with his Subjects in that quality, & such as then had no right to trade to the Indies, because of the laws & restrictions they lay under: for otherwise by keeping to the precise words of a Treaty we should quite lose the intent of it. As, for example, if the States of Brabant & Flanders should stipulate by a Treaty with the States General that the Zeelanders should be no more allowed to fish on the Coasts of Flanders, & after this promise made, the States General should allow the Hollanders to fish there. Or, which is the same thing, & contrary to the nature of all reciprocal Contracts, that the United Provinces should be excluded from all the western Coasts & from all the Spanish Islands in the East-Indies, but on the other hand what was yielded to us by the King of Spain might be taken away when ever he pleased; not indeed by Spaniards but by others of his Subjects, who they nearer they are our neighbours the more they can doe us prejudice, as well in the Indies as here at home in Europe. Surely if the contract had been made thus, or if the States could have foreseen that there would be a time, when by a nice distinction such injustice might be done, & that by distinguishing between the different qualitys of a Prince, & the different Subjects of either party, that great article of the Treaty of Munster might become of no use to them: 'Tis not to be supposed they would have made peace on such fallacious terms, or that they would have joyned at the beginning of this Century, in the Grand Allyance for recovering of the Netherlands to his Imperial Majesty, so as to bring a fatal mischief on themselves & their Subjects. Wherefor every body must judge our cause, who ask only to be no losers, & desire nothing but that our good offices may not be turned to our prejudice, juster than theirs who have no thing but gain in view; for there's great difference betwixt people who only endeavour to keep possession of their own, and others who by a new pretension demand a share of our Commerce, tho' they have contributed nothing to the establishing of it.

VIII. Mr. *Neny* pretends that even the King of Spain himself, *Charles* the II last deceased, did not understand it thus. But on the other side we have already affirmed with due respect, that not only the King, of Spain but even his Imperial Majesty too seem'd some years ago to understand it thus. As to the King of Spain, we gave constant use and an inviolable observation of the Treaty even Ref. Sect. 4.

 to

tempora, *& intaminatam fœderis observantiam. Respectu vero Cæsareæ suæ Majestatis idem præsumendum putavimus ex clausula quadam, quam commeatibus, quibusdam Belgii incolas à Cæserea sua Majestate antehac concessis, insertam vidimus*, quâ prohibentur Navigare & Commercia exercere ad illas Regiones, ubi subditis Cæsareæ suæ Majestatis secundum fœdera navigare & Commercia exercere non licet, *aut, ut verba Gallica se habent*: dans les endroits où il n'est pas permis, suivant les Traités, aux sujets de S. M. I. &c. de commercer. *Quæ clausula nobis ad Fœdus Monasteriense respicere visa est, quoniam nullum aliud Fœdus, quo hujusmodi verba sano sensu referri possint, usquam extat. Et primum quidem, nempe tales commeatus à Cæsarea & Cath. Majestate reverâ datos esse, non diffitetur* D. Neny Refut. suæ § ult. *sed consequentiam quam inde deducimus, prædicta nimirum verba ad Fœdus Monasteriense respicere, omnino negat, dum putat hanc clausulam supervacuam esse, & in casu, quo scripta est, nihil aliud efficere, quàm* quod clausulis istiusmodi, quæ Commeatibus vulgo inseri solent, Navarchi, *ut ait*, prohibentur colludere cum Piratis, aut cum hostibus Principis illius, qui talem Commeatum concessit. *Atque ita* Commercii *verbum ad* Piratas, Fœderis *nomen ad* Hostes *refert; & quando, si Diis placet, cum Jurisconsultis loquitur, affirmat, Principis verba in casu quo scripta sunt, nihil operari, & sine effectu accipienda esse. Sed quoniam nostrum non est, tantas componere lites, missa hac faciemus. Quid enim senserit Augustissimus Imperator, aut quid omnino non senserit, ipsa illa Majestas optime noverit. Nobis ex factis Summorum Principum aliquid conjectare licet, at de internis cogitationibus judicare nos non oportet.*

Nec magis etiam nostra referre putamus, quid senserit Glor. Mem. Carolus II. Hisp. Rex, quum vidimus quid fecerit, & appareat hunc Principem Fœdus Monasteriense religiosissime observasse: quamquam & hoc negare conatur D. Neny § 2. Refut. suæ, *ubi loquitur de quodam Privilegio, quod alte memoratus Rex, anno* 1698. *Belgii incolis concessisset ad navigandum ultra Europæ limites ad Indiarum tam Orientalium, quam Occidentalium oras, quod tunc temporis typis publice editum, & omnibus etiam Directoribus utriusque Societatis Fœderati Belgii innotuisse asserit; quos tunc non objecisse, ait, Fœdus aliquod, quod huic Privilegio obstaret, sed unice P. P. D. D. Ordines rogasse, ut lex conderetur, quâ Belgii Fœderati incolæ prohiberentur hujus novæ Societatis consortes & participes esse. Unde concludit, quod si Hisp. Rex scivisset sibi fœdus aliquod obstare; aut si P. P. D. D. Ordines simile quid cogitassent, nec ipse Rex ejusmodi Privilegium concessisset, nec P. P. D. D. Ordines contenti fuissent nudo Edicto, ne subditi sui hujus novæ Privilegiatæ Societatis participes fierent; sed Regem, ut oportet, solenni ritu certiorem fecissent, tale Privilegium cum fœdere non convenire. Quod quum factum non sit, inde probare conatur, Regem, & P. P. D. D. Ordines tunc temporis non existimasse illud Privilegium fœderi Monasteriensi adversari. Verum quid de hac re statuendum sit, dictu nobis difficile est; quandoquidem nemo nostrum tale Novum Regis Hispaniarum Privilegium unquam vidit, vel antehac fando de eo*

to this day as a sufficient proof: And we thought we might presume the same of his Imperial Majesty from a certain clause in Passports granted by his Majesty to some people in the Netherlands, where they are forbid to exercise any trade or Commerce to those parts which are prohibited by the Treaties. Or as it is in the French, *dans les endroits où il n'est pas permis, suivant les Traités, aux Sujets de S. M. I.* and this clause seemed to us to relate to the Treaty of Munster: for we don't know of any other Treaty which these words can possibly be apply'd to. That such Passports have been granted by his Imperial Majesty Mr. *Neny* does not deny, but our consequence that the forementioned words must relate to the Treaty of Munster he will by no means allow, and thinks that clause to be superfluous and of very little signification in the place where it stands, and only such as is generally inserted in the like Passports to hinder Masters of Ships from holding any correspondence with Pyrates or with the enemies of those Princes who have granted such Passports. So that he makes the word *commerce* relate to Pyrates and the word *Treaty* to Enemys. And when forsooth he takes upon him to talk like a Lawyer, he affirms that the words of the Emperour in this very case as they are here are of no manner of effect and signifie just nothing at all. But because tis not for us to determine matters of this nature we'll drop it here. His Imperial Majesty best knows what he meant or meant not on this occasion: Tis not for us to judge of the meaning of great Princes, we are to take our measures from their Actions only. Sect. Ult. Ref.

Neither is it our business to seek after the meaning of the said Charles II. King of Spain, since there appeared in all his actions a strict observance of the Treaty of Munster: altho' Mr. *Neny* would deny this, where he speaks of a certain Privilege which that King granted in 1698 to the Spanish Netherlanders, allowing them to Navigate both to the East and West-Indies; which Privilege he affirms to have been printed and publish'd at that time, and to have been known to the Directors of both the Companies of the United Provinces; which Companies notwithstanding (says he) never alledg'd any Treaty which oppos'd the said privilege; neither did they demand any thing more of the States, but that a Law might be made to prohibit the Dutch from being Members or sharers in this new Company: from which he concludes that if the King of Spain had known of any Treaty which restrained him; or the States thought any thing like it; the King would not have granted such a Privilege, nor would the States have been contented with a bare Edict, only restraining their Subjects, from being Sharers in that new privileg'd Company; but would in a publick manner have remonstrated to the King that to grant such a privilege was not agreable to the Treaty: from the not doing of which our Author would infer, that neither the King nor the States at that time, thought the granting of such a Privilege to be contrary to the Treaty of Munster. What to judge of this matter we cannot tell, for as much as none of us ever saw any such new Privilege of the King of Spain, nor till now ever heard Ref. S. 2.

quicquam audivit: in Actis etiam D. D. Ordinum & Societatis Indiarum Orientalium ne verbum quidem de eo reperitur. Et sicut certum est alte memoratos D. D. Ordines de re quam ignorabant, Edictum facere non potuisse, ita ex proœmio ejusdem edicti, quod huc adducit D. Neny, *evidentissime apparet, illud occasione hujusmodi Privilegii datum non esse, sed occasione renovati Privilegii Societatis Indiarum Orientalium, & prorogationis ejusdem ad Annum* 1740. *quando leges & statuta ad hanc Societatem pertinentia, more antiquo in compendium redigi & promulgari solent, quod tunc iterum* Append. No. II *factum esse, ipsissima edicti verba, quæ infra exhibebimus certo, certius denotant.**

Non diffiteor tamen, me dum hæc scriberem, copiam talis Privilegii, de quo loqui videtur D. Neny, *ab Amico ex Brabantia consecutum esse. Sed quum hoc, quod mihi videre nunc contigit, ab Rege subscriptum non sit, nec datum Madriti, sed Bruxellis, magis videtur illud a Regio Senatu Bruxellis, quam ab ipso Rege in Hispania datum esse: Saltem illud constat, prædictum Privilegium, qualecumque sit, executioni nunquam mandatum esse. Unde præsumendum est, illud semper in tenebris latuisse, ob defectum vel vitium aliquod, quo laboravit, vel ob aliam quamcumque causam, cujus rationem nos non tam facile reddere possumus, quam ex iis, quæ Articulo primo ejusdem Privilegii leguntur, evidenter demonstrare, Auctores illius non existimasse incolas Belgii Hisp. ratione commerciorum ad Indias, fœderis Monasteriensis plane immunes esse; adeoque illud fœdus non ita flocci fecisse, ut nunc facit* D. Neny, *qui ne ipsos quidem Hispanos clausula finali* Art. V. *amplius teneri contendit; sed eosdem omnino statuisse, Belgii Hispanici incolas hac in parte una cum Hispanis pari jure esse habendos; quoniam* dicto art. *illis nihil aliud concedunt, quam* ut navigare liceret & commercia exercere, ubicunque ipsis secundum fœdera inter Hisp. Regem & alios Europæ populos, ac speciatim quidem inter prædictum Regem & Provincias Unitas, navigare & commercia exercere liceret; *sic enim verba se habent:*

Que ladite Compagnie s'établira sous le titre & nom de Compagnie Royale des Païs-Bas, negotiant aux places & lieux libres des Indes Orientales & de la Guinée, où il leur est permis de naviger & negocier, sans contrevenir aux Traitez de paix, que nous avons avec la France, l'Angleterre, les Provinces-Unies, & autres Princes & Etats de l'Europe.

Agnoscunt igitur Fœdera, quæcunque Rex habebat cum aliis Gentibus, & speciatim cum Unitis Provinciis, quoad navigationem & commercia ad Indias, iisque Belgii incolas, non minus quam Hispanos obligari statuunt. Nam aliàs fœderum mentionem non fecissent, sed permisissent prædictis incolis longe lateque navigare, quocunque liberet; quippe quibus nulla lex vel fœdus obstabat; at contra illos limitant & restringunt ad loca libera, id est talia, quæ secundum Fœdera cum aliis Europæis populis

* Si quis pleniore super hac re demonstratione indiget, adeat ipsam *Resolutionem*, quod vocant. PP. DD. Ordin. Gener. quam, infra exhibemus in Appendice. No. III.

of it; neither is there the least mention made of it in the Journals of the States, or of the East-India Company. And as 'tis certain that the said States could not make an Edict upon what they knew nothing of, so it appears evidently from the Preamble of that very Edict here mentiond by Mr. *Neny*, that it was not made upon the account of any such Privilege, but on occasion of renewing the Privilege of our East-India Company, and prolonging of it to the year 1740. at which time the Laws and Statutes made in favour of the said Company, are usualy epitomis'd and publish'd; and that this was then done the very words of the Edict which we shall add at the end, infaillibly demonstrate.

But while I am writing this I have at last got a copy of such a Privilege as Mr. *Neny* seems to speak of, which is sent me from & friend in Brabant: But as it is neither signed by the King, nor dated at Madrid, but at Brussells, it seems very apparent that this Privilege was rather given by the Council at Brussells, than by the King of Spain: but however this is certain, that the said Privilege was never put in execution: and it is to be presumed, that it had never lain so long in the dark, unless there had been some fault or defect in it, or for some other particular reasons, which I shall not take upon me to explain: but I can safely undertake to prove from the I. Art. of this Privilege, that the Authors of it, whoever they were, did not think the Spanish Netherlanders to be entirely free with relation to the East-India Trade from any restraint by the Treaty of Munster, and by consequence that they did not make so light of that Treaty, as Mr. *Neny* would seem to do at present, who contends that even the Spaniards themselves are no longer bound by the last clause of the V Art. But the aforesaid Authors have plainly decided that the Spanish Netherlands in this case are upon the same footing with the Spaniards; for in the said Article there is no other Concession made them than to navigate and trade, wherever it might be allowed by the Treatys made betwixt the King of Spain and the other Nations of Europe, and particularly betwixt the said King and the United Provinces. The words are thus: *That the said Company shall be established under the name and title of the Royal Company of the Netherlands; and shall trade to such places or parts of the East-Indies or of Guinea where they may lawfully navigate and trade, without violating the Treaties of Peace, made by us with France, England, the United Provinces, or other Princes or States of Europe.* Append. No. III.

Thus they acknowledge the Treaties made by the King with the other Nations of Europe, and particularly with the United Provinces, with relation to the Navigation and trade of the Indies, and that the Netherlanders are no less bound by them, than the Spaniards themselves. For otherwise they had made no mention of a Treaties, but had permitted the said Netherlanders to trade every-where where they pleased, as people not restraind by any Law or Treaty whatsoever; but instead of that they limit and restrain them to such places as are free, that

* For a further proof of this we have also added the Resolution of the States General on this Matter. Append. No. II.

pulis libera sunt, quæque subditis Regis, salvis fœderibus, commerciorum causa adire licet. Ut jam porro restet inquirere, quanam hæc loca sint in Indiis Orientalibus, quæ respectu incolarum Belgii Austriaci pro liberis haberi possint.

CAP. II.

§. 1. Pro locis liberis haberi vult D. Neny *omnia loca à Societate Indiarum Orientalium nondum occupata, quæ sui juris sunt, & commercia cuivis gentium concedere possunt. At nos in hoc casu pro locis liberis habenda contendimus, quæ Regis Hispaniæ subditis, salvo fœdere, adire licet; ut jam quæstio propria sit, an prædicti subditi per fœdus Monasteriense tantummodo exclusi sint à locis Societati Fœderati Belgii propriis, an vero à toto tractu maris, quorsum Hispanos navigationem non extensuros clausulâ fin.* dicti art. 5. *Rex premisit.*

Diximus antea, Differ. nostræ *§. 6.* & 10. *Hispanis secundum sententiam Pontificis Maximi, (tanquam arbitri inter illos & Lusitanos) navigare non licuisse ultra Promontorium Bonæ Spei, nec ab Occidente ultra Philippinas Insulas, v. gr. ad Asiæ & Chinensium oras, ad tractum Cormandelicum, Bengalensem, Mare Rubrum, quæque his comprehenduntur. Sed aliud est, abstinere debere à certa parte maris, aliud à singulis locis ad alterum pertinentibus; nam quod meum est, eo ut meo uti possum, & jure dominii alios inde arcere, ad quod habendum & retinendum nec pacto, nec gratia aut consensu alicujus indigeo. Verum quandoquidem commercium Societatis Fœd. Belgii in Indiis Orientalibus tale est, ut minimum consistat in locis isti Societati propriis; quippe quæ præcipue servantur ad custodienda alia loca, aut tanquam horrea, in quibus merces per dissitas Indiarum oras collectæ reponuntur; quo pacto Batavia dici potest commune emporium totius Indiæ Belgicæ, non quia per se merces multas suppeditat, aut lucrum aliquod adfert, sed quia est quasi commune horreum & repositorium, quo merces undique coëmtæ coacervantur, & unde classibus quotannis in patriam deportantur; sic* Macasser, Timor, Ternate, *& alia loca, licet nullum commercium ibi detur, multo tamen milite & maximis impensis servantur ad custodiendas insulas aromatum. Quamobrem tali pacto cum Rege Hispaniarum percusso omnino opus erat, non ut Rex Privilegium nostrum confirmaret, sicut arguit* D. Neny *§.* 2. Refut. suæ, *quod, confirmata Republica, confirmatione non indigebat; sed ne Hispanis ad illam partem maris, quam Societas Fœderati Belgii commerciis suis jam occu-*

that is such as are allowed by the Treaties made betwixt the King of Spain and the other Nations of Europe, and which they, as his Subjects, observing those Treatys might freely trade to. So that it now remains only to be enquir'd, what places in the East-Indies with respect to the Austrian Netherlanders are to be accounted free.

SECT. II.

I. Mr. *Neny* is for having all those places reckon'd free which are not now in the actual possession of the East-India Company, or which have no dependance on any other, and can trade with any people they please. But we, in this case, maintain, that there are no other places to be reckoned free, but such, as the Subjects of the King of Spain are allowed by the aforesaid Treaty, to trade to. So that now the question properly is. Whether the said Subjects, by the Treaty of Munster, are only excluded from certain places belonging to the Company of the United Provinces, or from that whole tract of Sea, to which the King has promis'd by the last clause of the said 5. Art. to prohibit the Spaniards from navigating.

I have already said in my former Dissertation, that the Spaniards by the Sentence of the Pope (as Arbiter between them and the Portugeze) were not allow'd to navigate beyond the Cape of good hope, nor from the west beyond the Philipine Islands, that is to the Coasts of Asia, or of China, Cormandel or Bengal, to the Red sea, or to whatever places were comprehended under these. But tis one thing to be oblig'd to abstain from a certain part of the Sea, and another, only not to be allow'd to trade to particular places belonging to another. For what ever is already mine, I can make use of as my own, and by right of Soverainty keep it from all others; & to the having and holding of which I neither want the agreement, favour, or consent of any one. But the Commerce of the Company of the United Provinces, in the East-Indies is such, that it consists very little in the places that are properly their own, which are only kept as guards of other places, or as Storehouses for the Wares gather'd from the different Coasts of the Indies. Thus Batavia may be said to be the Common Mart of all the Dutch Indies, not for any considerable profit or merchandise which it affords itself, but because it serves by way of general Warehouse & repository, where the goods bought up on all sides, are gathered together, and ship'd off every year for Holland. So Macasser, Timor, Ternate, and other places, which yield nothing for Commerce themselves, are yet kept with many Soldiers and much charge to guard the spice Islands. For which reason 'twas necessary that such a Treaty should be made with the King of Spain; not that he should confirm our Privilege, as Mr. *Neny* would insinuate (for the Republick being once well settl'd, that wanted no confirmation) but that the Spaniards might not be allow'd to incroach upon those places where the Dutch had

Sect. VI. & X.

Ref. 5, 2.

occupaverat, navigare liceret, ultra quam tunc temporis propter supra memoratam Pontificis Maximi sententiam navigare erant soliti. Sunt enim commercia Societatis nostræ multorum commerciorum quasi una compages, sicut non male hæc descripsit S. Puffendorf, Introd. ad Historiam Europ. cap. 6. *licet huic Auctori omnia tam accurate noscere & desinire non contigerit, quàm res quidem exigebat.* Societas, *inquit*, Indiæ Orientalis maxime opes Reip. & commercia ingentibus accessionibus auxit: ea quippe oram illam longe lateque patentem, & opibus florentissimam, à Basora, ubi Tigris fluvius in Sinum Persicum evolvitur, usque ad extremas Japoniæ oras porrectam, commerciis frequentat: fœderibus cum multis Orientis Regibus juncta, & de monopoliis pactionem cum haud paucis eorum fecit: multa etiam loca munita tenet: Principem inter ea locum obtinet Batavia, in Java majore insula posita, Qui ibi degit, supremus Gubernator, seu Imperator, Regia fere pompa conspicuus, reliquis etiam Indiæ Provinciis præest. Eorum locorum summum imperium penes Societatem est. Inter ea eminent. Insulæ Moluccæ & Banda, Amboina, Malacca, ora Insulæ Ceylon, Paliacatta, Musulipatnam, Nagapatnam (ea regio in littore Coromandelico sita est) Cochinum, Canaor & Cranganor in littore Malabarico, aliaque.

Statuit igitur Vir Doctissimus, quod etiam rei veritate nititur, commercia hujus Societatis non consistere in locis propriis; sed præcipue in Commerciorum extensione quadam per dissitas Indiarum regiones intra limites Privilegii sui, quas stationibus, emporiis & tabernis instruxit, castellis ac fortalitiis munivit, coloniis ornavit, contractibus cum Indicis Principibus commerciorum causa sibi devinxit, & maximis sumtibus mercaturæ aptas fecit; ut si à locis propriis demantur commercia, quæ ad alias regiones & loca libera institui solent, loca ista non solum Societati nostræ plane infructuosa & inutilia fierent, sed praterea tam onerosa, ut relinquere ea, quam retinere, satius esset.

§. II. Atque hinc est, quod Directores Societatis Indiæ Orientalis, cum tempore Pacis Monasteriensis a PP. DD. Ordinibus consulerentur, quo potissimum pacto, ratione commerciorum Indiarum Orientalium cum Hispanis agendum esset, non suaserint, ut Hispani se tantummodo à locis Societati nostræ propriis abstinerent, sed ne navigationes suas ulterius, quam tunc navigare erant assueti, extenderent; id est, ut abstinerent a toto tractu maris, & ab omnibus locis ac regionibus in eo sitis, occupatis aut occupandis, nobis an aliis Principibus, aut etiam Lusitanis subjectis, sine discrimine; contra vero Societas nostra abstineret tantum a locis Hispanorum, quæ perpauca illi, & præter Manilhas *in India Orientali fere nulla tunc possidebant; adeo ut obligatio clausulæ finalis* d. art. 5. Pacis Monasteriensis, *non sit reciproca, ut nempe Hispani ita abstinerent a locis nostris, uti nos vicissim a locis Hispanorum; sed ut nos abstineremus a locis Hispanorum propriis, hi vero navi-*

had already a settled Commerce, nor to navigate beyond the limits assigned them by the forementioned decision of the Pope. For the trade of our Company is as it were a Chain of different trades link'd together: As it is not ill describ'd by Puffendorf; altho' his notions in several things are not so exact as might be. The „East-India Company, says he, has very much encreas'd the Riches and Com- „merce of the Republic, for its traffic is extended over all that large and wealthy „Coast, from Bassora where the Tigris empties it self into the Persian Gulph, e- „ven to the utmost borders of Japan: It has made leagues with many Eastern „Princes, and contracted with several of them for monopolising their commerce. „It has many Fortresses with Garrisons there, the principal amongst which is Ba- „tavia situated upon the Island Java. He who is Governor General there has an „attendance almost like a King, and has also the command of all the other Indian „Provinces; but the supream government of all is in the hands of the Company. „Among the other places the chief are the Islands of Molucca & Banda, Amboyna, „Malacca, the Coasts of Ceylon, Paliacatta, Musulipatnam, Nagapatnam, which „lies on the Coast of Cormandel, Cochin, Canaor & Cranganor, upon the Coast „of Malabar, &c.

Introd. ad Hist. Europ. Cap 6.

This Author then asserts, (which is certainly matter of fact) that the Trade of our Company does not consist in the places they are in possession of, but in a certain extended Commerce, thro' all the different countrys within the bounds of their Privilege, in which places they have made Havens, established Factorys, and places of resort, built Castles and Fortresses, planted Colonies, made Treatys with the Indian Princes on account of trade, and with extream cost and charge have adapted thing to their Commerce. So that if the places which we call our own should be depriv'd of their Commerce with those places, they would become not only altogether useless and unprofitable to the Company, but even so burdensome, that 'twould be much better to quit than to hold them.

II. And tis upon this account that the Directors of the East-India Company, at the time of the Treaty of Munster, when they were consulted by the States as to what might be necessary to stipulate with Spain in relation to the East-India trade, did not require that the Spaniards might only abstain from those places which properly belong'd to their Company, but that they should also be restrain'd from navigating beyond their accustom'd limits; that they should be excluded from all that tract of Sea, and all the Countries in it, which we were then in possession of trading to, or might be so afterwards, whether then subject to us, or to other Princes, without any distinction, or even to the Portugueze themselves: On the other hand that our Company should only abstain from the Places in the possession of the Spaniards, which places were then very few, or almost none at all, in the East-Indies, except the Manilhas. So that the obligation in the last clause of the said 5 Art. of this Treaty of Munster is not in such manner reciprocal, as if the Spaniards were only to abstain from our places, as we we were to abstain from theirs; but that we should abstain from the places

 possest

navigationes suas ulterius unquam extenderent. Ceduntur enim a Rege Hisp. Societati Belgii Fœder. non tantum oppida, fortalitia, castella & agri, quos tunc possidebant; sed etiam ea, quæ non possidebant, quæque in posterum illæso fœdere erant acquisituri, cum commerciis ad ea spectantibus. At, ne quis dubitet, an ista Hispanis interdicta navigationis extensio etiam referri debeat ad ejusmodi loca, quæ sui juris sunt, quæque commercia aliis quibuslibet gentibus concedere possunt; nec non ad Indias Lusitanorum; ne scilicet Hispani Lusitanos, tunc temporis Reip. nostræ, & illorum hostes, in Indiis armis persequendo, limites nostros invaderent, ac commercia nostra deteriora redderent. Videantur, quæso, Consultationes prædictorum DD. Directorum, quas una cum responso Legatorum Hisp. Regis exhibui Dissert. nostr. §. 11. *ubi apparet de unaquaque re separatim diversis articulis actum esse; & quidem* articulo primo *a DD. Directoribus rogatos esse PP. DD. Ordines, ut* curarent, ne Hispani navigationes suas commercii causa in Indiis Orientalibus ulterius extenderent; *altero* ut ab Indiis Lusitanorum etiam abstinerent, *quas Indias postea dict. art. 5. nobis cesserunt; (quatenus nempe loca quædam à Lusitanis recuperare possemus): Regis quoque Legatos ad singula separatim tunc respondisse, & quidem ad primum;* durum esse Regem impedire velle, commercia exercere ad ea loca, quæ libera essent, & quæ commercia aliis gentibus concedere possent. *Ad alterum;* iniquum fore, si Rex impediretur progressus facere adversus Lusitanos, *quos* rebelles *appellabant. Quæ expressa de utraque re separatim facta mentio, & congruens Legatorum responsio, luce meridiana clarius ostendit prohibitam illam navigationis extensionem, non solum referri debere ad Indias Lusitanorum, ne scilicet Hispani sub prætextu belli contra Lusitanos gerendi, limites nostros & commercia infestarent; sed etiam omnino referenda esse ad Indias, tam nobis, quam aliis Principibus subjectas, item ad loca libera, quæve sui juris sunt, & commercia aliis Gentibus concedere possunt, modo Fœdere & Privilegio Societatis Fœderati Belgii sint comprehensa. Ad quæ omnia Hispaniarum Rex dicto art. V. pollicitus est, subditos suos navigationem commerciorum causa non extensuros, ultra quam tunc temporis navigare erant assueti. Quod etiam usus; qui optimus omnium Fœderum & pactorum interpres est, ad hanc usque ætatem confirmavit, & nos evidenti exemplo, quod non multo post Pacem Monasteriensem contigit,* Dissert. nostræ §. 6. *probavimus. Nempe cum sæpius memoratus* B. Brouwer *Hispano-Brabantus, anno* 1653. *tentasset ad oras Chinenses navigare, hoc illi interdictum fuisse; non quasi Chinense Regnum haud esset liberum, sed quia Hispani tempore Pacis Monasteriensis eo navi-*

posseſt by them; and that they should never extend their Navigation beyond their present limits. For the King of Spain granted to the Company of the United Provinces not only the Towns, Fortreſſes, Caſtles and lands of which they were then in poſſeſſion, but alſo whatever others they should thereafter poſſeſs or acquire, without violating this Treaty, with all the Commerce thereto belonging. But if any one should doubt, if by this prohibition, the Spaniards were reſtrained from trading with ſuch places as were free & independent, & at liberty to trade with any other Nation whatſoever; as well as from that part of the Indies poſſeſs'd by the Portugueze, where the ſaid Spaniards, making war upon thoſe Portugueze, at that time both our enemies and theirs, might invade our limits, and become detrimental to our Commerce; let him conſider the repreſentation of the aforeſaid Directors, which together with the anſwer of the King of Spains Embaſſador I have inſerted in my former Diſſertation, where it appears Sect. XI. that thoſe two different things were treated ſeparately in different articles: In the firſt, the Directors deſir'd that the States should take care to hinder the Spaniards from extending their Commerce farther in the Eaſt-Indies; and in the other, that the ſaid Spaniards should alſo abſtain from thoſe parts of the Indies poſſeſſed by the Portugueze; which parts were afterwards granted to us by the ſaid 5 Art. (as far as we should recover them from the Portugueze): The Kings Embaſſadors alſo anſwered to each of thoſe Articles ſeparately; to the firſt, that it was hard that we should pretend to reſtrain the King from trading to ſuch parts as were free, and might trade with all other Nations; And to the other that it would be unjuſt to hinder the King from reducing to his obedience the Portugueze whom they called rebels. The mention of each of thoſe things being expreſsly and ſeparately made, together with the diſtinct anſwers then given by the Embaſſadors, make it as clear as noon day, that this reſtriction did not only relate to the Portugueze Indies [leaſt the Spaniards under a pretext of doing acts of Hoſtility there should infeſt our limits & hinder our Commerce] but likewiſe to all thoſe parts of the Indies, either in the poſſeſſion of us or other Princes, as alſo all free places which are independent and at liberty to trade with other Nations, as far as theſe places are included in the ſaid Treaty, and in the Privilege of the Dutch Eaſt-India Company: to all which places the King of Spain has promis'd in the ſaid V. Article, that his Subjects should not trade, nor extend their navigation beyond their accuſtomed limits. We have alſo prov'd in our former Diſſertation, that Uſe, the beſt interpreter of Treaties & Contracts, Sect. VI. hath confirm'd it to this time; and we have proved it by a very evident example, which happen'd not long after the Peace of Munſter: for when B. Brouwer a Spaniſh Brabander whom we have often mentioned, undertook in 1653. to navigate to China, he was hindered: Not becauſe China was not a free Coaſt, but becauſe the Spaniards did not uſe that navigation at the time of the Treaty of

navigare non erant assueti. Idem alio exemplo, extra hujusmodi fœderis vinculum, ex causa similitudine nuper demonstraverunt DD. Directores Societatis Indiæ Occidentalis,in Remonstratione, *quam anno præterito tradiderunt PP. DD. Ordinibus; scilicet cum Scoti, ineunte hoc seculo, in Regione Americana nomine* Darien, *sub prætextu, quod hæc Regio esset libera, & in ditionem Hispanorum nunquam redacta, coloniam construxissent, ad stabilienda ibi commercia sua, cum consensu & permissione incolarum, seu Domini loci; & Hispani Serenissimo Magnæ Britanniæ Regi contra ostendissent, hanc Regionem, quantumvis liberam, pertinere ad* dependentias *suas, (ut hoc verbo utar) quoniam unicum iter præberet ad commercia per terras cum utraque Americæ parte continuanda: quæ interrumperentur & ipsis infructuosa fierent, si Scotis ibi coloniam habere liceret; Alte memoratus Magnæ Britanniæ Rex, æquitate rei motus, non ægre tulit, ab Hispanis Scotos decedere recusantes, armis inde expulsos esse. Vide* l'Histoire du Roi Guillaume, livre. 8. p. 370. Item *Mercurium Europæum* ad annum 1700. mense Julio. *

§. III. *At mare & commercia libera esse oportere, ait* D. Neny, *neque Hispaniarum Regem ita subditos suos libertate naturali privare, aut fœdus cum alia Gente facere potuisse, quo minus ipsis navigare liceret, quocunque aliis Gentibus navigare, & commercia exercere liberum est. At nos jam ante monuimus, libertatem illam navigandi & commercandi non esse de absoluto hoc Jure Naturali, quod inter Gentes, quarum interest, legibus & fœderibus restringi ac prohiberi non possit; quod ex antiquioris ævi monumentis etiam plena exemplorum manu demonstrari posset, nisi hæc nostra ætas prohibitionum & restrictionum istiusmodi tantam copiam exhiberet, ut propterea ad antiquitatem recurrere operæ pretium non videretur. Imo, inquit* D. Neny, *acerrimus vester* Maris Liberi Vindex Grotius, *hic serio contradixit, contendens mari a nullo mortalium servitutem imponi posse, atque idcirco navigationes & commercia nulli posse prohiberi, præsertim ad loca libera;*

* Præter quæ D. Auctor hic adfert de Scotorum incepto in Isthmo *Darien*, notandum (quod non parvi momenti in hac controversia videtur) quamvis Scoti amplissimis Privilegiis muniti essent ad navigationes & commercia in Africam & utrasque Indias instituenda, & sibi licitum existimassent coloniam in isto loco libero ponere, cum nullum obstaret fœdus; Nihilominus Mag. Britanniæ Rex, audita hac de re gravissima querela Hispanorum, cum quibus pacem & amicitiam enixe colere voluit, non solum factum reprobavit, sed & ilico mandata dedit ad omnes suos subditos, præcipue in Coloniis Anglico-Americanis, ne quis eorum sub gravissima poena, Scotis, Coloniam illam contra pacem cum Hispanis, instruentibus, ullo modo faveret; nec illos concilio, auxilio, vel alio quocunque modo adjuvaret. Atque Mandata illa (quorum unum instar omnium in Apendice adjicimus) efficaciora fuere quam Hispanorum Arma, ad Scotos ab Isthmo *Darien* depellendos. Videatur etiam hac de re *Larrey Hist. d'Angleterre* &c. Tome IV. p. 828. 829.

Append. No. IV.

Munster. There is also another example which, altho' not done in consequence of a Treaty like this, yet from the similitude of the case, was made use of last year by the Directors of the West-India Company, in a Remonstrance delivered by them to the States (viz.) when the Scots at the begining of this Century had established a Colony at a place in America call'd Darien, with the consent and permission of the inhabitants and Lords of that place: tho' they pretended that it was a free country, as never having been under the subjection of the Spaniards, yet the King of Spain having remonstrated to the King of Great Britain, that that country, however free in it self, yet was a dependence of the countrys belonging to him, as being the only passage which his Subjects could make use of by land, to maintain the communication & Commerce between North & South America, which would be interrupted and quite broken off if the Scots should be allowd to settle there: The said King of Great Britain was so satisfied with the justice of the complaint, that he did not at all resent, that the Spaniards us'd force of Arms to oblige the Scots to leave the place. As may be seen in the *History of King William, lib. 8. p. 370.* as also in the *Mercury of Europe*, of July 1700.*

III. But, says Mr. *Neny*, the Sea and the Commerce of it ought to be free; and the King of Spain had no right to deprive his Subjects of their natural liberty, or to make a Treaty with any other Nation whereby they should be restrained from navigating to those parts where it was free for other people to trade and navigate. But we have before remark'd, that the liberty of navigating and trading, is not of such absolute natural right, as that it may not be prohibited and restrain'd by laws and Treatys made betwixt Nations concerned; which might be easily proved by a multitude of exemples from former ages, if the great quantity of such Prohibitions and Restrictions in our own times, did not make such a research unnecessary. But, says Mr. *Neny*, your own *Grotius*, a strong asserter of the freedom of the Sea, has formally contradicted such pretensions, and maintains, that no mortal has any right to restrain the freedom of the Sea, nor can therefore hinder any one from navigating and trading, especially to such places as

* Beside what our Author here relates about the undertaking of the Scots at Darien, it may be of some importance in this controversy to remark, that tho the Scots were fully authorised by their Patents &c. to establish their navigation & trade to Africa & the Indies both East & West, & thought they might lawfully settle a Colony in Darien, a free place & contrary to no Treaty; Yet a heavy complaint being made to K. William against it, from the Court of Spain, with which he was desirous to live in a good correspondence; he not only disowned the thing, but sent orders to all the English Plantations in America, that none should presume, on pain of the severest punishment, to hold any correspondence with the Scotch Colony erected in Darien, contrary to the peace between his Maj. & his Allies, or give them any assistance on any pretence whatsoever. As may be seen by that published in Jamaica, of which a Copy is here annexed. And these orders contributed more than the Spanish Arms to drive the Scots out of Darien. See on this matter the *Collection of State Tracts in K. Williams Reign*, Vol. III. pag. 494. &c. Append. No. IV.

bera, suique juris, quæve ab Europæis Gentibus nondum sunt occupata. Sed si Viro Clarissimo lubeat cognoscere, quid Grotius, *aliique nostri temporis celeberrimi JCti hac de re & senserint, & scripserint, ultro ab manibus istiusmodi conjectatiunculis abstinebit. Quid enim opus est ex incertis, aut ambiguis Grotii verbis conclusiones nectere, quum adire liceat atque consulere hunc ipsum Auctorem in notissimo opere* de Jure Belli & Pacis lib. 2. cap. 3. §. 15. *ubi ex professo hanc materiam (quando nempe res incidit in conditionem fœderis) tractavit, atque expressis verbis contrarium docuit; ita enim scribit:* Possunt enim ut singuli, ita & populi, pactis, non tantum de jure quod proprie sibi competit, sed & de eo quod cum omnibus hominibus commune habent, in gratiam ejus cujus id interest, decedere; quod cum sit, dicendum est, quod dixit Ulpianus in ea facti specie, qua fundus erat venditus hac lege, ne contra venditorum piscatio Thynnaria exerceretur, mari servitutem imponi non potuisse, sed bonam fidem contractus exposcere, ut lex venditionis servetur. Itaque personas possidentium, & in jus eorum succedentium obligari. *Assentitur hac in re Viro Maximo* Loccenius de jure maritimo lib. 1. cap. 4. n. 7. *Item* Leikherrus de jure maritimo cap. 7. & 12. *& novissime* Puffend. de Jure Naturali & Gentium, lib. 4. cap. 5. §. 10. *scribens hunc in modum:* Ex hisce liquet pacatam Oceani navigationem omnibus esse liberam, cum nemini adhuc tale jus in eum sit constitutum, ut cæteros inde arcere queat: & per legem humanitatis talem esse debere, adeoque neminem posse prohibere, quo minus populi Oceanum accolentes, ipsi non subjecti, inter se commercia instituant, nisi pacto tale jus sibi quæsiverit, ut, aut unus populus in ipsius gratiam certum quempiam populum a suis commerciis arcere teneatur, aut quia ipse cesserit facultate sua ad eum populum navigandi. *Et paulo post:* Hoc ipsum est libertatis, ut quis de jure suo alicui tertio per pactum cedere queat. *Et in fine istius §. 10.* Ita si v. gr. populus Europæus regionem aliquam Asiæ aut Indiarum suam fecerit eo modo, qui inter gentes Dominium parere solet, recte quoque, si videbitur, omnem aditum ad eandem commerciorum causa susceptum, cæteris poterit præcludere, aut non, nisi sub certa conditione, certove onere permittere. Id quod ita observari videmus, nec in eo quicquam apparet, quod naturali rationi repugnet. Nam illa tantopere jactata commerciorum libertas non obstat, quo minus civitas plus suis civibus, quam exteris favere queat.

§. IV. *Apparet igitur meridiani solis luce clarius, talia pacta omni jure licita esse, nec naturali juri adversari; sicut hodie etiam nihil frequentius est, quam ea inter populos quorum interest, & iniri & servari. Quare, si verum sit Regem Hisp. post Fœdus Monasteriense ejusmodi Privilegium, de quo loquitur* D. Neny, *dedisse; hoc saltem certum est, quod Rex de jure suo, aut de Indiis suis aliquid concedere au largiri potuerit, non autem de alieno, adeoque nec de Indiis, quas commerciorum causa nobis jam ante cesserat; quum hæc duo in uno eodemque actu minime subsistant,*

as are free, and independent, or to such as are not in the possession of any European Nation. But when this Gentleman comes to know what *Grotius* and other famous Lawyers of our own times have thought and wrote upon this subject, he'll abstain of course from trifling after this manner. For what occasion is there to draw conclusions from a few uncertain or ambiguous terms of *Grotius*, when we may go and consult the Author himself in his famous work de *Jure Belli & Pacis lib. 2. cap. 3. §. 15.* where he expresly treats of this matter (that is in cases of contract) and in express words teaches the very contrary. *Whole Nations*, (syas he) *as well as private persons, may renounce in favour of another, not only such rights as are peculiar to themselves, but also such as they have in common with others: and in that case we may say with* Ulpian, *in a case where land was sold on this condition, that the seller reserved entirely to himself the right of fishing* Tunne, *without allowing any such right to the buyer, that the liberty of the sea could not be restrained, but by the faith of the Contract it was necessary to keep to the condition of the Sale; & therefore the buyers or possessors were really bound to it.* With this great man agrees *Loccenius de Jure Maritimo*, Lib. I. Cap. 4. n. 7. as also *Leikherrus de Jure Maritimo*, Cap. 7. & 12. & likewise *Puffendorf de Jure Naturæ & Gentium* Lib. IV. Cap. 5. §. 10. where he says: *Hence it apears that the peaceable navigation of the Ocean is free to every one, since no man has yet got such a right to it that he may exclude others, & since it ought to be free by the laws of humanity: and therfore no man has a right to hinder people, not subject to him, living on the Sea coasts, to trade with one another; unless he has acquired by convention such a right, that one nation in his favour is bound to forbid all trade with another nation, or has yielded up to him its right of navigating to that nation.* And a little lower; *This is true liberty, that any one may by convention yield his right to another.* And at the end of this paragraph. ,,So if any European Nation has acquired the possession of any ,,country of Asia or the Indies, in such a way as dominion is usually acquired among ,,men, that nation may very justly if they please forbid all others to trade there, ,,or allow them only on certain conditions & with certain restrictions. This is what ,,we see commonly practised, nor do I see that it is at all unreasonable: For the ,,freedom of commerce so much cried up does not hinder any State from favouring ,,its own Subjects more than foreiners.

Nothing then can be more clear than that such Treatys are by all laws allowable; nor are they contrary to the law of nature, as we see by dayly instances of such Treatys made and kept by the different Nations that are concerned in 'em. Wherefore if the King of Spain after the Treaty of Munster, did grant such a Privilege as Mr. *Neny* speaks of, this at least is certain, that that King had a power to give or grant whatever he pleased of his own right, or of his own Indies, but nothing at all of what belonged to another; and by consequence none of

stant, Fœderis mentionem facere, & permittere, ut contra Fœdus navigetur. Absurdum itaque sequeretur, si obtinere deberet sententia D. Deny, *qui contendit per* loca libera *intelligenda esse loca sui juris, quantumvis ratione commerciorum secundum pacta conventa non amplius libera sint, & eatenus ad alterum, cui commercia eorum soli relicta sunt, pertinere intelligi debeant.*

Proinde, si Belgii Hispanici incolæ conatibus suis desistere nolint, & res (quod Deus quidem avertat) aliter expediri nequeat, non culpandæ forent Societates Fœd. Belgii, si armis, juris sui servandi gratia, uti cogerentur. Neque Cæsarea sua Majestas hoc ægrius ferre posset, quam Magnæ Britanniæ Rex illud tulit, dum subditos suos a Darien *decedere nolentes ab Hispanis vi armata expelli passus est. Nec objicere quis poterit cum Nobili Germano, qui nuper de hac eadem re scribens, ex Grotio* de Jure belli & pacis lib 1. cap. 3. §. 4. *perperam allegavit,* læsæ Majestatis teneri, qui injussu Principis bellum gesserit, delectumve habuerit, excercitum comparaverit. *Nam si Vir ille nobilissimus pariter retulisset, quod laudatus auctor* d. l. *subjungit in Notis*, videndum esse, an tales subditi acceperint Imperii Summi partem, aut a Principe acceperint Privilegium se muniendi ac tuendi, & suis viribus aliquid copiolarum ad defensionem alendi; *& ipse, & alii cognovissent illud, quod Grotius ibi refert, per* l. 3. ad l. Jul. Majest. *nec pertinere, nec referri posse ad Societatem nostram, cui omnes actus Summi Imperii, & speciatim etiam armorum usum in Indiis ad defensionem sui exercere, amplissimo Privilegio est concessum; quod cum propter causam onerosam datum sit a Principe, nec adimi, nec minui potest. Præterea actum defensionis pacem non rumpere, & injuriam facere non videri qui jure suo utitur, notissimi juris est.*

CAP. III.

§. *I. Pergimus nunc ad tertium tædiosæ hujus controversiæ caput, cujus materia quo illustrior, eo nobis molestior est. Etenim porro inquirendum est, utrum Cæs. & Cathol. sua Majestas Belgicas Provincias possideat pari jure & modo, quo Augustissimi ipsius Majores eas possederunt ante ætatem Philippi I. cognomento* Pulcri; *an potius Alte memorata Cæs. & Cath. Majestas easdem nunc possideat, sicut novissime defunctus Rex & Belgii Princeps Carolus II. eas possederat, nempe cum iisdem oneribus, juribus, commodis & incommodis, quæ Principes ante ipsum hisce Provinciis imposuerunt.*

Quod ad prius attinet, illud affirmare videtur D. Neny Refut. §. 1. *dum ait;*

Les

those Indies which he had before yielded up to us for our Commerce: for it can never be consistent in the same Act, to mention a Treaty to be observed, and at the same time to permit such Navigation as is directly contrary to the said Treaty. It would be absurd then to allow what Mr. *Neny* pretends, that by free places, are to be understood, such as are of themselves independent, when in relation to commerce, by foregoing Treaties they are not free, but in that regard belong to such only as are permitted to trade to them.

Therefor, if the Netherlanders will not desist from their undertaking, and matters (which God forbid) cannot be accommodated otherways; the Companies of the United Provinces cannot be blam'd if they are oblidg'd to make use of arms to defend their right. Nor can his Imp. Majesty have any more reason to resent this, than his Brit. Majesty had when he suffer'd that his Subjects should be driven away from *Darien*, by the Arms of the Spaniards. Nor can that be any objection which a German Gentleman, lately writing on this matter, has very improperly alledg'd from *Grotius de Jure Belli & Pacis*, Lib. 1. cap. 3. § 4. *That he is guilty of Treason, who makes war, levys men, or raises an army without his Princes order.* For if he had also related what that Author subjoins in the notes [viz] that it ought to be considered, whether such Subjects had obtained any share of the Soverain power, or were authorised by any Privilege from their Prince to arm, and defend themselves, or to maintain Troops for their defence, both he and every body else would have seen, that *L.* 3. *& L. Jul. Majest.* which Grotius quotes here, does not in the least touch the case of our Company, to whom are granted, by a most ample Privilege, all the Acts of Sovereignty, and particularly, the use of arms for their own defence in the Indies; which since granted by the Sovereign for onerous causes, can not be taken away now nor diminish'd. Moreover to act in ones own defence is no breach of peace; and that he does no body injury who only makes use of his own right, is a known Maxim in law.

SECT. III.

I. I come now to the third head of this ungrateful dispute, the matter of which is so much more difficult to handle, as tis of greater consequence. And here we are to enquire whether his Imperial Majesty possesses the Netherlands by the same right and in the same manner, as they were possessed by his Ancestors before Philip I. Or whether his said Majesty possesses them only as they were possessed by their late deceased Sovereign K. Charles II. that is with all the rights, burdens, advantages & disadvantages which the Princes before him had brought upon them.

Mr. *Neny* seems to affirm the first, when he says. „The stipulations made &

 agreed

Les stipulations faites & arrêtées par les differents articles des Traités, dont on vient de parler, établissent d'une maniere incontestable, que les Païs bas Autrichiens sont unis à perpetuité aux Etats de la Très Auguste Maison en Allemagne, & que Sa Majesté ne les possede en Souveraineté & proprieté, que comme Souverain & Proprietaire desdits Etats, & comme Chef de ladite Maison, & consequemment de la même maniere, que ses Augustes Ancêtres les avoient possedés avant l'avenement de Philippe le Bel à la Couronne d'Espagne.

Quod dum statuit, incidit in tempus Maximiliani I. memorati Philippi Parentis, cujus conjugio cum Maria, Caroli Audacis filia unica, Belgicæ Provinciæ primum ad Domum Austriacam devenerunt; licet hæc ad Cæs. & Cath. Majestatem nullo modo referri po at; quoniam Maximilianus I. hasce Provincias nunquam acquisivit, nec possedit tanquam verus seu naturalis Dominus, sed tanquam Dominus dotis, atque ita post mortem uxoris non suo, sed tutorio nomine illas administravit. Certum etiam est Cæs. & Cath. suam Majestatem non successisse Maximiliano I. sed Carolo II. cujus heredem illum futurum fuisse, si Rex ille intestatus decessisset, atque hoc nomine Testamentum illius Regis oppugnasse, bellum indixisse, Regiones & Urbes occupasse, ex Confœderatione Magna, ex belli indictione, aliisque actis tam liquido constat, ut illud hactenus inficias ierit nemo. Errat itaque D. Neny, *cum tam indistincte arguit Cæs. & Cath. suam Majestatem hasce Provincias possidere, sicut Illustrissimi illius Majores illas possederunt ante Philippi Pulcri ætatem, quoniam Majorum nullus ante hanc ætatem eas possedit, præter Maximilianum I. cujus possessio cum illa, quam Cæs. & Cath. sua Majestas nunc obtinet, minime convenit. Nam si hæc statuas, & cum* D. Neny *affirmare velis, Cæs. & Cath. suam Majestatem non possidere tanquam Burgundiæ Ducem, & Successorem Caroli II. sed tanquam Austriæ Ducem, aut Successorem Maximiliani I. ad hanc absurditatem devenies, ut omnia Pacta & Fœdera, quæ Burgundiæ Duces, veri harum Provinciarum Domini, a Philippo Pulcro usque ad Carolum II. cum aliis Gentibus fecerunt, & omnes illorum Actus, imo ipsum Fœdus Monasteriense nullius esse dicas momenti. Atque ita tota possessionis causa, contra expressum Fœdus Antverpiense, mutabitur: quò tamen temerarius Nobilis cujusdam Germani calamus nuper admodum inconsiderate erupit, cum hac falsissima ratione ausus fuerit libertatem Reip. nostræ in controversiam vocare, & Majestatem ipsius publice impugnare, in libello, cui titulus:* Grundliche Erweisung von Ihro Kayserlichen Majest. habendem Rechte zu Aufrichtung einer Ost-und West-Indischen Compagnie in dero Oesterreichischen Niederlanden &c, §. 15. p. 29. *ubi ineptissime arguit,* Prædictum Fœdus Monasteriense a linea agnatica juniore Augustissimæ Domus Austriacæ nunquam approbatum fuisse; adeoque eo non obligari Cæsaream suam & Cath. Majestatem, junioris hujus lineæ superstitem unicum agnatum. *Quin eo etiam temeritatis prorebitur, ut Diploma, quod brevi post Pacem Monasteriensem dederat Gloriosissimus Imperator Ferdinandus III. super* Attic. 53. *ejusdem Pacis, rogatu scilicet Hispaniarum Regis,*

de

„agreed on by the different articles of the Treaties which we have been speaking „of prove undeniably that the Austrian Netherlands are united for ever to the „States of the most illustrious House of Austria in Germany, and that His Imp. Ma„jesty does not possess them otherwise, but as Sovereign and proprietor of the said „States, and chief of the said House, and by consequence in the same manner as „his Ancestors possess'd them, before the accession of Philip the Fair to the Crown „of Spain.

What he says here must be referr'd to the time of Maximilian I. Father of the said Philip, by whose mariage with Mary, the daughter of Charles the Bold, the Netherlands came first into the House of Austria; tho I don't see how this can have any relation to his Imperial Majesty; because Maximilian I. never acquired the said Netherlands, nor ever possessed them as true and natural Lord, but in right of his wife; and so after her death he govern'd them as Guardian, and not as Lord. 'Tis certain also that His Imperial Majesty does not succeed to Maximilian the I. but to Charles II, whose Heir he was to be if he had died without a Will. And that it was in this right that he oppos'd the Testament of the said King, declar'd war, seiz'd Countries & Cities, is plain by the Grand Alliance, & other acts, & is what no body till now has ever doubted. Mr. *Neny* therefore is out, when he talks so undistinctly of his Imp. Majesty's possessing those Provinces as they were possessed by his Ancestors before *Philip* the Fair, because none of his Ancestors before that time ever had possession of them, except Maximilian I. whose possession was very different from that of the present Emperour. And if you hold with Mr. *Neny*, that his Imp. Majesty does not possess the Netherlands as Duke of Burgundy and Successor of *Charles* II. but as Duke of Austria or Successor of Maximilian I. you must fall into this absurdity, that all the Contracts and Treaties, which have been made with other Nations by the Dukes of Burgundy, the true Sovereigns of the said Provinces, from Philip the Fair down to Charles II. as also all their Acts and even the Treaty of Munster would be of no force. And so the whole foundation of his Imp. Majesty's right would be chang'd, against the express Treaty of Antwerp. Which nevertheless has been rashly and inconsiderately urg'd by a certain German Gentleman, who has presumed by this false reason to call in question the liberty of our Republick, and openly to attack its Sovereignty, in a book under this title: *Grundliche Erweisung* &c. or, *A demonstration of the Right that his Imp. Majesty has to erect an E. & West-India Company in the Austrian Netherlands.* §. 15. p. 29. where he very silily argues, *That the aforesaid Treaty of Munster was never approv'd of by the younger branch of the House of Austria, and by consequence does not oblidge his Imperial Majesty who is the only surviving heir of that line.* Moreover he goes to that height of impertinence to pretend that the Act given, at the desire of the King of Spain by Ferdinand III. a little after the Peace of Munster, upon the 53. article of that Treaty, about maintaining friendship and neutrality with

de bona amicitia & neutralitate cum P. P. D. D. Ordinibus conservanda, *susque deque habendum esse*, ibidem *satis proterve contendat: hac etenim verba ejusdem diplomatis:* dictumque Articulum, ejusque contenta, quatenus ea ad nos pertinent, pro nostra parte approbaverimus, ratificaverimus &c. *tantummodo ad Imperatoriam Majestatem, non vero ad Augustissimam Domum Austriacam, vel Romanum Imperium pertinere affirmat; unde hunc in modum concludere non dubitat:* An Fœderatum Belgium ex tacita agnitione, & quasi possessione libertatis, contra pætensiones Imperii & Augustissimæ Austriacæ Domus, præscriptione (velut communi exceptione) jure se defendere possit, alii judicent. *Verum, quid Vir Nobilissimus per* Imperatoriam Majestatem, *hic intelligat, nisi Supremum Imperii & Augustissimæ Domus Austriacæ in Germania Caput, fateor me non intelligere: & ne ipsum quidem me capere profiteor, qua Jurisprudentia Imperator, qui unum Articulum Fœderis, ad quem consensus & gratia ipsius requirebatur, expressis verbis distincte, & sine ulla Protestatione agnovit, & approbavit, non etiam intelligi debeat totum Fœdus approbasse, si illud approbatione indiguisset; aut, quando quis approbavit aliquid,* quantum ad se pertinet, & pro parte sua, *illum non approbasse etiam pro posteris suis atque successoribus; præsertim quum res ipsa declaret, hæc verba,* quatenus ea ad nos pertinent, *non ad exclusionem descendentium, sed ad aliam rem spectasse. Nam cum* Art. 53. *duæ res requirerentur, nempe Consensus Imperatoris intra duos menses, & Imperii Germanici intra anni spatium, Imperator ideo consentit* pro se, & pro parte sua, *(non ut seipsum, aut descendentes eo excluderet) sed ne consentire videretur pro Imperio Germanico, cujus consensus seorsim requirebatur.*
Apend.No. V. *Sicut hæc ex ipsissimis Diplomatis verbis, quod infra exhibetur, luce meridiana clarius apparet.*

§. III. *Præterea, si totum Fœdus Monasteriense sedulo perscruteris, ad nullum ejus Articulum approbationem Imperatoris, aut Germanici Imperii requisitam esse deprehendes, nisi ad hunc unum Articulum 53. quo tamen ipso, si verba recte inspiciantur, non requiritur Approbatio Fœderis, verum ut Imperator & Imperium ad hoc Fœdus tanquam tertii accedant,* ad bonam amicitiam atque neutralitatem cum Fœderato Belgio colendam; *quod benigne etiam ab Imperatore promissum est, secundum verba ejusdem Diplomatis, quæ summatim ita se habent.* Nos, re mature ac diligenter deliberata, pro singulari & propensissimo nostro in pacem quaquaversum promovendam ac propagandam studio, in ejusmodi petitionem clementer annuimus, dictumque Articulum, ejusque contenta, quatenus ea ad nos pertinent, auctoritate nostra Imperiali approbamus &c. *Quamobrem hæc verba,* quatenus ea ad nos pertinent, *longe aliud innuere videntur; nempe totum Fœdus Monasteriense ad* Lineam Agnaticam Domus Austriacæ in Germania, ad Imperatorem, *vel ad Imperium, excepto hoc uno articulo, nihil omnino pertinuisse; adeoque Hispaniarum Regem, ut illud Fœdus cum Fœderatis Belgis iniret consensu hujus lineæ non magis indiguisse,* quam

the States, is to be reckon'd of no value, for he affirms that these words of that Act (viz.) *We for our part have approv'd and ratified, the said Article and whatever it contains as far as it relates to us* &c. Are only to be understood of His Imperial Majesty as such, but that the Archduke of Austria and the Roman Empire are in no manner concern'd in the affair: after which he is pleased to add. *I leave to others to judge if the United Provinces have a good right, from a tacit allowance & precarious possession of liberty, to defend themselves by prescription, as a sufficient reason, against the pretentions of the Empire & of the most illustrious House of Austria.* But what this Gentleman here means by His Imperial Majesty, as separate from the head of the Empire and chief of the House of Austria, I must confess I don't well understand. I would also fain know by what Law, the Emperor, who distinctly, in express terms, and without any scruple acknowleg'd and approv'd one article of a Treaty to which his favour and consent were requir'd, should not be understood also to have approv'd the whole Treaty, if it had wanted his approbation; and likewise when any one approves any thing, *as far as it relates to him and for his part,* whether he does not also approve it for his Successors and posterity; especially when the thing it self makes plain that the words, *for as much as it relates to us,* did no way concern posterity, but were us'd upon quite another account. For since the 53. Art. requir'd two things (viz) the consent of the Emperor within two Months, and that of the German Empire within a year; the Emperor consented in these terms, *for himself and for his own part;* not that his Successors should not be supposed likewise to consent to it, but because he should not seem to consent for the German Empire, whose consent was also separately required. This appears clearly from the very words of the said Act, which we shall give at the end of this Dissertation. Apend. No.V.

III. Moreover if you examine the Treaty of Munster you'll find that there is no other article in the whole Treaty which required the consent of the Emperor or the Empire except this 53 Art. alone. Nor does this itself, if the words are nicely examin'd, require an approbation of the Treaty, but that the Emperor and Empire should concurr as Thirds, *for the maintainance of friendship and neutrality with the United Provinces;* which was freely promis'd by the Emperor in the words of the said Act, the substance of which is thus. *We after diligent and mature deliberation, and for our singular and extream desire of promoting and maintaining peace on all hands, do graciously agree to a petition of this nature, and approve with our Imperial Authority, the said Article and whatever it contains, as far as it relates to us* &c. So the words, *as far as it relates to us,* seem to have quite another signification [viz] that no other part of the Treaty of Munster, except this Article alone, had any manner of relation to the younger branch of the House of Austria in Germany, to the Emperor or to the Empire; & therefore the King of Spain had no more

occa-

quam V. gr. frater aut cohæres aliquis, cui familiæ erciscundæ judicio fundus obtigit, ad alienandum illum postea alterius quendam cohæredis aut agnati consensu indiget. Erant enim Hispaniarum Reges a Philippo I. usque ad Philippum IV. dicti Fœderis auctorem, tam pleni Belgii Domini, ut ad ipsam Provinciarum alienationem tam Matrimonii, quam Hæreditatis jure, nullius nisi Procerum consensu indiguerint. Nam si Ferdinandus III. tanquam Lineæ Austriacæ in Germania Caput & Princeps, tunc temporis jus aliquod habuisset, propter quod hoc pacis Fœdus in detrimentum ipsius ratum esse non posset, solenni ritu ipsum protestatum fuisse oportuerat, ne sciens & tacens jus suum remittere videretur. Jam vero quandoquidem hujusmodi protestatio facta non est, sequitur totum illud Fœdus, præter hunc unum articulum, ad lineam agnaticam Domus Austriacæ non pertinuisse. Quantum vero ad Romanum Imperium attinet, verum quidem est Imperat. Carolum V. aliquando hasce Provincias eidem Imperio, Burgundici Circuli nomine adjunxisse, hac tamen conditione, ut suis propriisque legibus regerentur, & ad onera, quæ requirebantur ad communem defensionem, tantum contribuerent, quantum duo Electoratus. *Sed recte a Puffendorfio observatum est, hanc conjunctionem brevi post sponte evanuisse, & omni fere effectu caruisse, quum ait* in Libro de statu Imp. Germ. Cap. 2. §. 4. Sed quæcumque ratio subegerit, ea conjunctio fere effectu carere visa fuit, nisi quod Burgundiæ nomine in Comitiis suffragium fertur; nam ita ample Belgarum libertati cavendum fuit, ut tota illa incorporatio ad solam fere causam tributorum, quæ pro communi tutela Germaniæ essent necessaria, adstringeretur; quæ &c. ipsa tamen Belgæ conferre abnuerunt; ac vicissim Germaniæ Ordines nunquam se obligatos crediderunt ad partem bellorum Belgicorum capessendam, velut ad se nihil spectantium. *Unde etiam sequitur, Imperii consensum ad Art. 53. non alium in finem requisitum esse, quam ut bona neutralitas inter Imperium & Fœd. Belgium coleretur, quemadmodum etiam Imperatoris consensum requisitum esse supra diximus. Denique etiam Majestatem Reipublicæ ab ipso Ferdinando III. deinceps semper agnitam esse, nec non ab Imperio Germanico & Membris Imperii, imo ab ipsa Cæsarea & Catholica sua Majestate, atque ab Augustissimis illius Majoribus, infinitis actibus probari posset, si id probatione indigeret quod nunquam in dubium vocatum a quoquam fuit.*

§. IV. Sed ne tempus teramus respondendo hujusmodi argutiis & subtilitatibus, quæ (ut recte doctissimus Gronovius ad Grotii lib. 2. Cap. 7. §. 27. de jure Belli & Pacis *notavit) omnem bonam fidem de Fœderibus summorum Principum tollunt; redeamus ad id, quod proprie ad rem nostram pertinet; qui hic non agimus de jure Domus Austriacæ, aut Germaniaci Imperii, sed de jure Ducum Burgundiæ,*

qui

occasion for the consent of this other branch towards the making of the Treaty of Munster with the United Provinces than (for example) a brother or coheir to whom an estate is finally adjuged with the consent of the family & others concerned, has occasion for their consent in selling it afterwards: For the Kings of Spain from Philip I. down to Philip IV. with whom the said Treaty was made, were so absolutely Lords of the Netherlands, that to alienate them either by Mariage or Heritage, they wanted nothing but the consent of the States. For if Ferdinand III. had, at that time, as Prince and Chief of the branch of Austria in Germany, any right which could have hinderd the ratification of the said Treaty to his detriment, he ought formally to have protested against it, least by wilfull silence he might seem to quit his pretensions. But seeing there was no such protestation made, it follows that no part of this Treaty, except this article alone, any way concern'd the younger branch of the House of Austria. As to what relates to the Roman Empire, tis true indeed that the Emperor Charles V. once united those Provinces to it, and call'd all together the Circle of Burgundy: but upon this condition that the said Provinces should be still govern'd by their own Laws, and should contribute to the common defence as much as two Electorates. But tis justly observed by Puffendorf that this union was of very little effect, and in a short time vanished of its own accord; he says in his book *de Statu Imp. Germ. c. 2. § 4. But, what ever might be the reason, this union seemd to be almost of no effect, except giving a vote in the Diet of the Empire for Burgundy, for there was so much care taken of the libertys of the Netherlanders, that this incorporation seem'd to be made only that they might contribute to the common safeguard of Germany as there was occasion for it, which yet the Netherlanders refused to do, as the States of Germany in their turn did not think themselves oblidg'd to take part in the wars of the Netherlands, as not at all concern'd in them.* From whence it follows that the consent of the Empire to the said 53 article was no farther requisite than to preserve a good neutrality betwixt the Empire and the United Provinces; for which reason the consent of the Emperor was also required, as we have said before. As for the Soveraignty of our Republick, it would be easy to prove by numberless documents, that it was always acknowledged, after the Treaty of Munster, by the said Emperor Ferd. III. & by the Empire & the different Members of the Empire; & also by his present Imp. Majesty, as well by his most illustrious Predecessors, if such a thing wanted proofs which was never yet called in question by any body.

IV. But not to lose time in answering such Cavillings and subtileties, which as Gronovius in his notes on *Grotius* has well observed, are only fit to destroy all the faith which is due to the Treaties of Princes, let us return to the matter in hand, for 'tis not our business to dispute about the rights of the House of Austria or of the German Empire, but about that of the Dukes of Burgundy, who were

De Jure Belli & Pacis lib. 2. cap. 7. § 27.

qui quondam Belgii Principes fuerunt, & quorum postremo Carolo II. Cæs. & Cath. Majestas, non tanquam Austriæ, sed tanquam Burgundiæ Dux Duci successit; quod quum aliunde satis probari possit, restat ut hic tantum inquiramus, an jus illud hæreditarium, seu successionis, respectu Cæs. Majestatis ac Fœderatarum Potestatum, quarum intererat, quodammodo mutatum sit, sive per bellicam occupationem, sive per Confœderationem, aut per transactionem, vel aliam quamcumque rem, quæ post obitum Caroli II. acciderit.

Certe, si Principum res privatorum causis assimilare nobis liceret (quia ut ait Imperator in l. 4. Cod. de LL. illorum auctoritas a juris autoritate pendet, & digna Majestate Imperantis vox est, alligatum legibus se Principem profiteri.) *nos istam hæreditatis, & successionis seu possessionis causam, respectu Cæs. & Cathol. suæ Majest. per armorum interventum, seu bellicam occupationem, de jure non magis mutatam putaremus, quam si, v. gr. privatus aliquis, lite mota, hæreditatem, quæ ipsi debebatur, acquisivit; qui creditoribus defuncti & aliis quorum interest, objicere nequit, se istam bonorum possessionem non obtinuisse jure hæredis, sed ex causa judicati, vel ex pacto, si forte, pendente lite, inter cohæredes de ea re transactum fuisset, quoniam, sicut in privatis causis sententia judicis, & pacta seu transactiones jure hæreditario nituntur, & hujusmodi pactionibus cohæredes ab oneribus hæreditatis non liberantur; quin unusquisque eorum creditoribus, pro parte quam ex hæreditate consecutus est, maneat obligatus, haud secus ac si judicatum vel transactum non fuisset; ita in hoc casu omnis armorum usus, & bellica occupatio, nec non pacta seu transactiones de hac hæreditate facta, eodem jure nixa fuerunt. Quamobrem ad majorem cautelam articulo I. tractatus de* Barriere *expresse id actum conventumque est, ut* Cæs. & Cathol. sua Majestas hasce Provincias possideret, sicut postremus Hisp. Rex & earum Provinciarum Princeps eas possederat, aut possidere debuerat; hoc *est cum omnibus juribus oneribus commodis & incommodis, sicut tempore mortis ejusdem Regis fuerunt. Nec imputandum est* PP. DD. *Ordinibus, quod rerum humanarum vicissitudine coacti, Cæs. & Cath. Suæ Majestati non omnia pro voto conficere potuerunt; præcipue cum Magna Confœderatio ista conditione facta non fuerit, ut, nisi debellatum esset, ac Cæs. & Cathol. Sua Majestas tota hæreditate potiretur, omne id, quod a parte Cæs. & Cathol. Suæ Majestatis in favorem Magnæ Britanniæ Regis & Fœderati Belgii repromissum erat, irritum foret, verum ut illud præstaretur, si non in omnibus omnino Hispanicæ Monarchiæ ditionibus, saltem in terris quas belli fortuna recuperare liceret; id quod liquidissime probatur per ipsum prædictæ Confœderationis Instrumentum, quo id inprimis actum est*, ut Fœderati Principes operam darent, ut C. S. M. via amicabili & per transactionem, aut si hac non succederet, par arma, æquam & rationi convenientem satisfactionem in causa memoratæ successionis ob-

formerly Sovereigns of the Netherlands, and to the last of which, Charles II. succeeded his present Imp. Majesty, not as Duke of Austria but of Burgundy, which may be sufficiently prov'd in another place, so what remains for us to inquire is, whether that hereditary right or Succession, with respect to His Imperial Majesty and such of his Allies as are concerned, hath been any way changed, either by Wars, Alliances, Transactions or any other thing whatsoever that has happen'd since the death of the said Charles II.

And if we may compare the affaires of Princes with those of private men (because as Justinian says, *Their Authority depends upon the authority of the Law, and tis a saying worthy of the Majesty of a Soverain to acknowledge himself tho' a Prince yet to be oblidg'd to observe the laws*) we may be certain that the nature of inheritance, succession or possession, with respect to his Imp. Majesty, by the intervention of War or Arms, is no more chang'd in equity, than if (for example) any private man was to sue for an heritage and recover it by law, & should afterwards object to the Creditors of the deceased, or others concerned, that he does not now possess those goods in right of inheritance, but by the decision of the Court, or perhaps from some convention or contract made between the parties whilst the suit was depending: For as in private cases, the sentence of the Court, as well as agreements or treaties are founded on hereditary right, & the Coheirs by such agreements are not freed from the burdens that lay on the inheritance, but on the contrary every one of them remains bound to the creditors for the share he has of that inheritance, in the same manner as if there had been no sentence or no agreement: So likewise in this case all the use of Arms & possession by War, as also all the Contracts and Treatys made about this Succession are founded on the same right: For which reason in an article of the Barriere Treaty it is, for the better security, expresly stipulated and agreed, *That His Imp. & Cath. Majesty should possess those Provinces as they were or ought to have been possessed by the last King of Spain their Soveraign*, that is with all rights, incumbrances, advantages & disadvantages, as they were at the time of the said Kings decease. Nor is it to be imputed to the States, that by the vicissitude which all human things are subject to, they were not able to do so much for His Imp. Majesty as they desir'd; especially seeing the Grand Alliance was not made upon the condition, that, unless all was conquered, and His Imperial Majesty put in possession of the whole inheritance, all the promises made by his said Imp. Majesty to the King of Great Britain and the States of Holland should be void; but on the contrary that all should be performed as it was agreed on, if not in all the parts of the Spanish Monarchy, at least in such of them as they should have the fortune to recover. And this is clearly prov'd from the very Treaty of the Grand Alliance, where tis especially covenanted, that *the Allies shall do their endeavour, that His Imp. Majesty, in a friendly way and by Treaty, or if that don't succeed, by Arms, may obtain a just and reasonable satisfaction with regard to the said*

obtineret, atque ut vicissim Magnæ Britanniæ Regi & DD: Ordinibus securitas sufficiens præstaretur, pro custodia finium suorum, atque ut Navigatio & Commercia sarta tecta fervarentur; *sicut hoc latius demonstratum est Dissert. nostræ, §. 15. & 16. & porro apparebit ex Fœdere Antverpiensi, vulgo dicto* Tractatu de Barriere, *inter Cath. & Cæs. S. M. & Serenissimum M. Britanniæ Regem ac PP. DD. Ordines die 15. Novemb. ann. 1715. facto; quippe quo præcipua illa capita, quorum intuitu Confœderatio Magna erat inita, nempe* Securitas finium & Commerciorum, *Sereniss. Magnæ Britanniæ Regi & DD. Ordinibus renovantur & confirmantur, ac statim in Proœmio ejusdem Tractatus repetitur:* ut Belgii Hispanici Provinciæ Confœderatis Potestatibus essent pro obice & propugnaculo, non tantum ad mutuam defensionem, sed etiam ad conservationem Commerciorum suorum. *Et art. 26.* Ut Commercia & quæcunque inde dependent, in totum & per partes, inter subditos utriusque Belgii subsistant eo statu & modo, quo illa subsliterunt, & stabilita fuerunt per articulos Fœderis Monasteriensis, anno 1648. inter Glor. Mem. Regem Philippum IV. & PP. DD. Ordines initi, qui articuli, quantum ad commercia pertinent, isto tractatu denuo confirmantur. *Sic etiam articulo 22. ejusdem Tract. Cæs. & Cath. S. Majestas* æs alienum defuncti Regis PP. DD. Ordinibus solvere recepit: *pluraque alia ab eo profecta sunt, quæ uti hic recensere longum foret, ita luce meridiana clarius demonstrant, illud successionis jus, quo Cæs. & Cath. sua Majestas Belgicas Provincias acquisivit, respectu Fœderatorum Principum, quorum interest, mutatum non esse occupatione bellica, vel transactione, aliove pacto contrario, quo minus scilicet Alte Memorata Majestas Fœderum antiquorum effectum iisdem Principibus præstare teneatur, non secus ac defunctus Rex, si vixisset, ad illius præstationem fuisset obligatus.*

Sed objicit hic iterum D. Neny: *Quoniam commodum* Art. 5. Pacis Monasteriensis *est penes Hispaniarum Regem, tanquam Indiarum possessorem, eundem Regem etiam incommodum sequi oportere, & durum quidem esse, Belgii Austriaci incolas incommodis Fœderum onerari, qui commoda nulla exinde percipiunt. Sed respondemus ad Belgii Austriaci incolas commoda Indiarum nunquam pervenisse, quamobrem nec incommoda hodie sentire possunt: Si qui vero sint, qui grave damnum & incommodum sentiant, esse Societates Privilegiatas Fœderati Belgii, quæ ab una parte Hisp. Regi manent obligatæ, ab altera parte omne jus suum & commercia ad Indias, una cum Privilegiis interire vident. Nam si Belgii Austriaci incolis liceat quaquaversum limites Privilegii nostri Commerciorum causa frequentare, atque in Indias navigare, modo abstineant a locis nonnullis, quæ Societas nostra tanquam propria possidet, ratio ex pari iniquitatis causa postulat, ut idem concedatur incolis Fœderati Belgii; ut nempe civibus nostris, potius eadem liber-*

Succession; and that sufficient security be given to the King of Great Britain and the States of Holland for defence of their frontiers, and the preservation of Assert. 3.
their Navigation and Commerce; as is prov'd more fully in our Dissertation; it Sect. XV. & XVI.
may be seen also in the Treaty of Antwerp commonly call'd the *Barrier Treaty*, made Nov. 15. 1715. betwixt his Imp. Majesty, the King of Great Britain, and the States of Holland, for there the Principal heads, with view to which the Grand Alliance was made, (*viz. the security of their frontiers & their commerce:* are renew'd and confirm'd to the said King of Great Britain and the States, as 'tis recited in the Preamble of the said Treaty: *That the Spanish Netherlands should serve as a Barrier to the Allies, not only for their mutual defence, but also for the preservation of their Commerce.* And Art. 26. *That their Commerce and whatever depended on it, in whole or in part, should continue between the inhabitants of both the Netherlands, in the same way and on the same foot, that it was settled and regulated by the articles of the Treaty of Munster in 1648. between K. Philip. IV. of happy Memory, and the said States, which articles so far as they relate to trade are again confirm'd by this Treaty.* So by Art. 22. of the same Treaty, *His Imp. Majesty has taken upon him to pay the debt of the said deceas'd King to the States.* There are many more things that have followed upon this, which it would be too tedious to relate here, that yet prove very clearly, that that right of Succession by which his Imp. Majesty is possess'd of the Netherlands, with relation to the Allies therein concern'd, has no way been chang'd, either by War, or Transaction, or by any Contract, so as his said Imp. Majesty can be releas'd from the performance of former Treaties made with the said Princes, any more than the deceas'd King could be, if he were still alive.

But Mr. *Neny* objects here again; That because the K. of Spain has possessions in the Indies & enjoys the benefit of the V. Article of the Treaty of Munster, he ought also to bear the inconveniencies of it; but that it would be hard to burden the Netherlanders with the inconveniencies of the said Treaty, seeing they receive no manner of benefit from it. But we answer; that the said Netherlanders never enjoyd any benefit from the Indian trade, and therefore can not now be said to suffer any loss in being depriv'd of it: and if any are to complain of considerable losses and inconveniencies, 'tis the Companies of the United Provinces that have most reason; since on the one hand they remain oblidg'd to the performance of the Treaties made with Spain, and on the other they are depriv'd of their Rights, their Commerce and their Privileges. For if it were reasonable to allow the Netherlanders to navigate to the Indies, and to trade every where within our limits, abstaining only from those Places which our Company possesses in property, it would be every whit as reasonable that such an allowance might also be made to the inhabitants of the United Provinces, or that this liberty were

libertas detur, quam allenigenis; atque hi suo, potius quam Brabantorum nomine, & recta via magis quam per ambages (ut nunc fit) eadem Commercia una cum Brabantis exercere permittatur, quando brevi actum fore de Privilegiis nostris, nemo non videt

Atqui abstinere se dicunt prædicti Belgii Austriaci incolæ in Indiis Orientalibus a regionibus & locis, quæ commerciorum causa a Societate Privilegiata Fœd. Belg. tenentur. Sed si hoc verum sit, rogo, quid igitur fecerint in Mari Rubro? quid ad Malebaricum? quid ad Cormandelicum littus? quod utrumque castellis, oppidis munitis, tabernis & stationibus nostris fere totum occupatur. Quid in ostio Bengalensi, & emporiis sub Imperio Magni Mogolis? Ad quem legatio a Societate nostra nuperrime missa, Privilegiorum & contractuum cum illo Principe renovandorum gratia, eidem Societati constitit circa 240000 *Ducatis aureis, sive floren.* 1300000. *Quid ad oras Chinenses? Quorsum Hispanis a tempore Pacis Monasteriensis navigare nunquam licuit? Quid ad Insulam Ceylon, & alia loca? Ut nihil hactenus intentatum reliquerint, præter Aromatum Insulas & pauca oppida, quæ quidem sunt in Dominio Societatis nostræ, sed tam immenso oneri habentur, ut una cum dependentiis suis per totam Indiam Belgicam quotannis, sine gravissimis impensis* 150000 *Ducatorum aureorum sive* 750000 *flor. custodire & conservari nequeant. Sed quamvis ea, quæ diximus, tam vera sint, ut ab ipsis exercitoribus & navium magistris, qui nuper Ostenda ad Indias navigare cœperunt, negari non possint, mirifice tamen detorquentur a* D. Neny: Refut. suæ §. 3. *sequentibus verbis.*

Ces Societés ont des Isles & païs aux Indes, qui leur appartiennent en proprieté, du commerce desquels elles excluent toutes les autres Nations, à cause que les possessions qu'elles y ont, sont privatives, dans lesquelles les sujets de l'Empereur ne les ont jamais troublées, & ne les troubleront jamais dans la suite.

Elles ont en outre des Châteaux, factoreries, & loges au Royaume de Bengale, sur les côtes de Cormandel, sur celles d'Afrique & ailleurs, où les Anglois, les François & d'autres Nations Européenes en ont aussi, où elles font pareillement un Commerce privatif, dans la possession duquel les Habitans des Païs-Bas Autrichiens ne les inquietent pas; c'est de quoi les Directeurs devront tomber d'accord.

Il est vrai, que les Directeurs disent, que les sujets de l'Empereur ont trafiqué, & trafiquent encore dans des districts, qui seroient dependants de leurs places, Châteaux & loges, & que ce Commerce leur seroit défendu aussi bien, que celui de leurs dites places Châteaux, & loges: la raison en est, que comme le Commerce des Places principales appartient privativement aux dites Societés, à l'exclusion de tous autres, il s'ensuit de-là, que le Commerce

granted to our own Subjects rather than to Strangers; as also that they might be allow'd, to take part in this new Commerce, under their own names rather than under the names of Brabanders, and to follow the business directly, rather than by indirect means as they do at present: And if this were so every body may see that in a little time our privileges would come to nothing.

But if the Netherlanders say, that they abstain from all those countries and places in the East-Indies which are held by our Company on the account of trade; Pray what business have they in the Red sea? What upon the coasts of Malabar or Cormandel, which are almost all full of Castles, Fortresses, Lodges and Havens of our Companie? What have they to do in the Gulf of Bengal? or in the trading places in the Moguls Country? to whom there was an Embassy sent very lately by our Company for the renewing of the Privileges and Contracts made with that Prince, which cost the Company near 240000 Ducats, or 1300000 Florins. What brings them to the Coasts of China where the Spaniards were never allow'd to trade since the peace of Munster? What brings them to the Island Ceylon, and other places? For at present they have left no part unatempted, but the spice Islands, and a few towns, which indeed are in the possession of our Company, but are so prodigiously chargeable, that they together with their dependencies in the Dutch Indies cannot be kept and guarded without a yearly expence of 150000 Ducats, or 750000 Florins. But altho' what we here relate be so true that it cannot be denied by the Ship Officers and Masters themselves, who have lately begun to navigate from Ostend to the Indies; yet Mr. *Neny* has taken great pains to represent it otherwise in the following words.

These Companies have Isles and Countries in the Indies, which are properly their own, from the Commerce of which they exclude all other Nations, because these Possessions are for them alone, and in those the Subjects of the Emperor have never yet, nor will hereafter molest them.

They have also Castles, Factories and Lodges in the Kingdom of Bengal, and on the Coasts of Cormandel, as well as in Africa, &c. where the English French and other European Nations have possessions likewise, where they trade exclusive of all others; there the Netherlanders doe not disturb them, as the Directors themselves cannot deny.

Tis true the Directors say that the Subjects of the Emperor have traded and continue to trade to those places which are within their districts and which are dependancies of their settlements Forts, and Lodges, and to which they have as little right to trade, as to the settlements, Forts and factories themselves; and the reason is, that since the Commerce of the principal places belongs absolutely to them exclusive of all others, it follows that they have the same right exclusive in other places which are dependencies of the said principal ones, because their right in those dependencies of their Fortresses is as good and effec-

merce de leurs dependances leur appartient aussi privativement, à cause que leur droit dans les dependances de leurs Forts est aussi bon & aussi efficace, que celui qu'elles ont dans les Forts mêmes.

Mais il est aussi vrai, qu'ils ont fourni par ce discours l'occasion de faire voir clairement, que leur raisonnement est Sophistique, & se reduit à une vraye illusion.

Car posant pour constant, que les dependances des places, Forts, & loges desdites Compagnies leur appartiennent en propre, comme leurs établissemens principaux, & qu'elles ont un Commerce privatif dans les dites dependances au même titre, que le Negoce de leurs places, Châteaux & Loges, leur appartient privativement, il s'ensuit de là d'une maniere concluante, que les sujets de sa Majsté Imperiale, n'ont jamais commercé dans aucuns districts, Havres, ou Rivieres, qui sont des dependances des places, & habitations des dites Societés, puisqu'ils n'ont trafiqué jusque à present, & ne pretendent jamais trafiquer, que dans les endroits où les François, les Anglois, & d'autres Européens commercent librement &c.

Sermonem hunc satis esse perplexum, & cum rebus ipsis ac factis parum convenientem, facilius ignoscere possumus, quam silentio id præterire, quod hoc loco utique monendum est, Anglos nempe & Gallos, cæterasque Europæas Gentes, veluti Lusitanos & Danos, in regno Bengalensi, & in tractu Cormandelico, Commercia non exercere in locis nostris, aut ubi nos stationes habemus, sed in locis duntaxat, quæ illi populi antiquitus in his oris, permittente Principe, obtinuerunt, & possederunt. Quare argumentum, quod auctor ab his desumsit, ad alias Gentes, quæ eo nunquam navigaverunt, aut Commercia illa exercuerunt, minime procedit; nedum hoc procederet ad talem Gentem, quæ expresso Fœdere una cum Hispanis ad abstinendum est obligata, quæque ad illas oras nunquam navigavit, ac per diversa Fœdera insequentia prohibita est, quoniam omnia Pacta & omnes Confœderationes cum Cæs. & Cathol. Majestate eo pertinuerunt, ne scilicet in terris a Rege Hisp. antea possessis, & in ditionem Cæs. & Cathol. suæ Majestatis redigendis, novi aliquid induceretur, quo Commercia nostra deteriora fierent in Indiis, vel alibi, quod latius Differt nostr. §. 15. & 16. *demonstravimus.*

Præterea, quamvis concedamus illud, quod Auctor hic dicit Vers. Il est vrai, *nempe* illum qui obtinet castrum, etiam jure sibi vindicare posse omnia commercia & emolumenta, ad illud castrum spectantia, quum in dependentiis non minus juris habeat, quoad commercia, quam in ipso castro, *quod latius affirmat Solorz.* de jure Indiarum lib. 3. cap. 3. n. 40. & seqq. *atque etiam constat ex art*: 5. Pacis Monast. *ubi per Regem Hisp. ceduntur non tantum* loca, castella, oppida, *sed etiam* commercia ad illa loca, Castella, &c. spectantia; *negamus tamen Societatem Privilegiatam Indiarum Orientalium hoc argumento unquam usam esse, quoniam nos non agimus de commerciis particularibus, ad hæc vel illa loca aut castra*

spectan-

effectual, as their right in the Fortresses themselves.

But it is also certain that by this discourse they have given occasion for any one to see clearly, that their reasoning is nothing but sophistry and illusion.

For allowing it certain that the dependencies of their settlements, Forts and Lodges belong to them as properly as the Forts themselves, and that they have a right of commerce, in the said dependencies, exclusive of all others, by the same title that they have such right in their settlements, Forts and Lodges, it follows evidently that the Subjects of His Imp. Majesty have never traded to any districts, Havens or so manner depending on the places or Forts settlements of the said Companies, since they have never yet traded or pretended to trade, to any other places, than to such, as the French, English, and other people of Europe trade to freely &c.

One may easily pardon the perplexity of this discourse, & its unfairness in misrepresenting of facts, & pass it by in silence; but 'tis necessary in this place to remark that the English, French, or other Nations of Europe, as the Portugueze and Danes, do not trade in Bengal, or upon the Coasts of Cormandel, to any of our places, or where we have any settlements, but only to such places on these Coasts as they have formerly obtain'd and possess'd by the permission of the Inhabitants. Wherefore the argument which our Author has drawn from the practice of these Nations is good for nothing as tis apply'd to others who never had any trading or navigation to those parts; nor can it be at all apply'd to a People who along with the Spaniards were oblig'd by an express Treaty not to trade to those parts, who never did trade thither, and were by several subsequent Treaties prohibited from it: For all the contracts and Alliances made with His Imp. Majesty have had this in view, that nothing new should be introduced in those parts before possessed by the King of Spain, and to be reduced to the subjection of His Imp. Majesty, which might be detrimental to our Commerce in the Indies or elsewhere; as we have prov'd more fully in our first Dissert. Sect. XV. & XVI.

Moreover, altho' we may grant what our Author says in that paragraph, *'Tis true &c.* (viz.) That he who has got a Fort may at the same time justly claim all the Commerce and emoluments belonging to that Fort, since his right as to Commerce is no less in the dependencies than in the Fort it self; which is more fully asserted by *Solorzanus de Jure Indiarum*; and is also manifest from the V. Article of the Peace of Munster, by which the King of Spain yielded not only the Places, Forts, & Towns, but also all commerce belonging to the said Places, Forts &c. yet neverthelesss we deny that ever the Dutch East-India Company has made use of this argument; because the dispute here is not for particular trading to this or that place or settlement, but for the general trade of that whole tract of Sea, in which the Spaniards were forbid to navigate: And this Mr. *Neny* himself doesnot deny, when he says; *that tis agreed on and stipulated*

L. III. Cap. 1. n. 40. & seqq.

Refl. 5.

 by

ſpectantibus, ſed de univerſalibus, quæ ſcilicet ſpectant ad totum tractum maris, quorſum Hiſpanis Commerciorum cauſa navigare non licet; quod ipſe D. Neny §. 5. Refut. ſuæ *non diffitetur, quum dicit:* il eſt arrêté & conditionné par la clauſe finale du dit art. 5. que les Eſpagnols n'étendront pas leur navigation aux Indes Orientales, & que les Habitants des Provinces-Unies s'abſtiendront de frequenter les places poſſedées par les Caſtillans aux dites Indes, de ſorte que cette convention ne ſe borne pas à maintenir reſpectivement les parties contractantes dans leurs poſſeſſions aux Indes Orientales, comme il avoit été reglé auparavant par la dite ſeconde clauſe, à l'égard de toutes les dites Regions éloignées, mais ôte de plus aux Caſtillans la liberté d'étendre leur Commerce aux Indes Orientales, pour empêcher, qu'ils ne fiſſent des conquêtes ſur les Portugais, comme je l'ai déja obſervé. Mais comme ce retranchement de liberté eſt limité en termes precis aux Indes Orientales, & aux Caſtillans, on ne peut l'étendre, ny aux Indes Occidentales, ny aux Côtes d'Afrique &c.

Cumque nemo arbitrari poſſit, P. P. D. D. Ordines in gratiam Luſitanorum ita ſtipulatos fuiſſe, ut vult actor hic &, & §. 2. Refut: ſuæ, *nempe ad Indias illorum protegendas; præcipue ſi conſideretur, quod pax cum Luſitanis tunc nondum erat facta; contra vero tempus induciarum, anno 1641. inter illos & P. P. D. D. Ordines initarum, brevi erat exiturum; apparet ex his omnibus, auctores iſtiuſmodi ſophiſmatum, de quibus loquitur auctor, non fuiſſe DD. Indiar. Orient. Directores, ſed illos, qui talia ex vanis cogitationibus ſibi fingunt, & aliis temere perſuadere cupiunt.*

§. VI. Ultimo loco concludit D. Neny §. 6. Refut. ſuæ, *ex Negotiatione, quæ anno 1718. habita eſt Hagæ Comitis, ſuper articulis Tractatus* de Barriere (quibus agitur de ſolutione debitorum Belgii Hiſpanici) *PP. DD. Ordines tunc temporis in ea opinione non fuiſſe, quod nova iſta navigatio, quæ Oſtendæ erat inſtituta, Fœderibus adverſaretur*, quoniam, *inquit*, durante hac negotiatione, per totum biennium, de ea re a PP. DD. Ordinibus nulla mentio facta eſt, licet tunc naves nonnullæ Oſtenda ad Indias mitti cœpiſſent.

Sed reſpondemus ad hanc objectionem, verum eſſe quod ab anno 1715. uſque ad annum 1718. naves quædam Oſtenda ad Indias navigaverunt, duplici quidem commiſſione, nempe ad deprædandos hoſtes Cæſ. & Cath. ſuæ Majeſtatis, & ſimul ad commercia exercenda iis in locis, ubi ſubditis Cæſ. & Cathol. Majeſtatis, ſecundum Fœdera cum aliis gentibus commercia exercere liceret. Sed quam primum erat compertum, ejuſmodi naves, quæ Flandrorum nomine tunc vela faciebant, iſta commiſſione Cæſ. & Cath. ſuæ Majeſt. abuti, & hoc obtentu in locis Indiarum Occidentalium negotiari, ubi ſubditis Cæſ. & Cath. ſuæ Majeſt. ſecundum Fœdera commercia exercere non licebat, una atque altera illarum navium a Societate Indiarum Occidentalium Fœderati Belgii capta eſt. Deinde cum etiam Societas Privilegiata Indiarum Orientalium comperiſſet, naves nonnullas ſimili modo ad Indias Orientales navigaſſe, & intra terminos ſui Privilegii commercia exercuiſſe; verum quidem eſt, Societatem iſtam ſuis Miniſtris in Indiis non ſtatim mandaſſe, ut ejuſmodi naves caperent, ſed ſolummodo interdixiſſe, ne huic novo atque illegitimo commercio faverent,

præ-

by the final clause of the said 5 Article, that the Spaniards *shall not extend their navigation in the* East-Indies, *and that the* Dutch *shall abstain from navigating to the places possessed by the* Castillians *in the said Indies, so that this contract does not only maintain the contracting Parties respectively in their bounds in the* East-Indies, *as it had been before regulated by the second clause, with regard to the said remote places, but it takes away from the* Castillians *the liberty of farther extending their* Commerce *in the* East-Indies, *to hinder them from making any* Conquests *on the* Portugueze, *as I have already observ'd. But since that restriction is in precise terms limited to the* East-Indies *and to the* Castillians, *it cannot be extended to the* West-Indies *or the* Coasts *of* Africa *&c.*

Now since no body can imagine, that the States would have stipulated in favour of the Portugueze, to protect their Indies, so as our Author pretends here, and in his 2. Section, especially considering that the Peace was not at that time made with the Portugueze, but on the contrary the Truce made in 1641 between them and the States was just about expiring; One may reasonably conclude from this & other arguments of our Author, that the *Sophistry & Illusion* which he is pleased to attribute to the Directors of the East India Company, ought rather to be attributed to such as having formed silly arguments in their own brain, are weak enough to think to pass them for curent on the world.

VI. In the last place Mr. *Neny* concludes, from his Negotiations at the Hague in 1718. upon those Articles of the Barrier Treaty relating to the payment of the debts of the Spanish Netherlands, that the States were not at that time of opinion, that this new Commerce begun at Ostend, was contrary to the Treaties, because, says he, for two whole years during this Negotiation there was not a word mentioned of it by the States, altho' the Ostenders had then begun to set out Ships for the Indies.

But we answer to this objection, that it is true indeed, that from the year 1715. to 1718. there were certain Ships sent from Ostend to the Indies with a double commission (viz) to take such Ships as were enemies to his Imp. Majesty, and at the same time to trade to such parts, as the Subjects of his said Imp. & Cath. Majesty, as well as those of other Nations were allow'd to trade to by the Treatys. But as soon as it was found, that some Ships of this sort sailing under Fleemish colours, had abus'd his said Imp. Majesty's Commission, by presuming under that pretence to trade to certain places in the West-Indies, where the Subjects of his said Imp. & Cath. Majesty were not allowed to trade by the Treaties, several of their Ships were taken by those of the Dutch West-India Company. Thereafter when our East-India Company found, that certain Ships under the same pretence had sail'd to the East-Indies, and traded within the limits of their Privilege; tis true, they did not give immediate orders to their Officers in the Indies to have such Ships taken, but only forbid them in any ways to favour this new and unlawful commerce, or to furnish the Masters of those ships with such necessaries, as they allowed to other European Nations lawfully trading thither;

præbendo scilicet navium magistris necessaria illa, quæ aliis Europæis populis legitime ad sua loca navigantibus præberi solent; & quæ nos subditis amicissimi semper Principis, in hoc casu, rerum nostrarum necessitate coactos, negare debere ex animo dolemus. Itidem cum prædicta Societas anno 1720. *certior facta esset, incolas Belgii Austriaci, non obstante hoc interdicto, navigationes & commercia sua continuare, armis quidem abstinuit, sed nihilominus imploravit auxilium a P. P. D. D. Ordinibus, petiitque, ut Illi tandem Cæs. & Cath. Majestati ostendere vellent, hanc navigationem cum Fæderibus non convenire: quod memorati DD. Ordines non abnuerunt, verum illud omnibus modis Cæs. & Cathol. Suæ Majestati ostendere & notificare non destiterunt; adeo ut hæc lenta, & per legitimos tramites, a parte Societatis Indiarum Orientalium facta oppositio, retardata non fit ob juris defectum, sed honoris duntaxat & reverentiæ causa, quam se Augustissimo Imperatori semper debere profitetur. Quamobrem etiam hujusmodi cunctationem juri suo minime fraudi fore sperat: nec causam se præbere existumat, quapropter merito objicere quis posset, peccare nos in officia humanitatis, secundum quod ex Cicerone lib.* 1. de Offic. *huc adfert Welwodus cap. ult.* de Domin Maris; quando fine detrimento suo quis potest alteri commodare in iis, quæ sunt occupanti utilia & danti non molesta, quidni faceret? *quum ita hæc res comparata sit, ut sine maximo detrimento omnino concedi non possit. Atque ut hoc exemplo uti nobis liceat, si Cæs. & Cath. suam Majestatem, cui salus subditorum suorum optimo jure cordi est, inutilitatem ipsorum cavere decuit* per art. 17. Tractatus Antverp. *ne in territorio D. D. Ordinum prope* Blankenberg *ab illorum subditis piscatio in mari exerceretur; quanto magis P. P. D. D. Ordines curare æquum est, ne Ostendæ, contra tot Fæderum intentionem, tam insignis navigatio instituatur, unde non tantum Privilegiatis Fæderati Belgii Societatibus, sed etiam Reipublicæ maximum detrimentum juste metu præsagiendum est?*

FINIS.

hither; and which they were heartily sorry, as the case stood, that they were, oblidg'd to deny to the Subjects of so good an Allie as his Imp. Majesty. And when the said Company in 1720 were further assured that the Netherlanders notwithstanding this interdiction, did continue the said Navigation and Trade, 'tis true they made no use of arms, but they begg'd the assistance of the States, and desir'd that they would remonstrate to his Imp. Majesty that this navigatioin was not allowable by the Treatys. Which the said States agreed to, and did accordingly by all manner of ways notify and remonstrate the same to his said Imp. Majesty. So that this slow and methodical proceeding of the East-India Company in opposing the said Commerce, was not delay'd for want of right on their side, but only thro' their great respect to his Imp. Majesty. Wherefore the said Company hopes that such a respectfull forbearance for a little time, will not diminish their right: neither do they think that they have given any just occasion for any one to judge them guilty in point of Humanity, according to that of *Tully l.* 1. *de Offic.* made use of by *Welwood*, in his last Chapter *de Domin. Maris*, *when any one without any detriment to himself can oblidge another with such things as may be of service to the receiver, and no injury to the giver, why should not he do it?* For the case here is such that we can yield nothing without a manifest detriment to our selves; and that I may be allow'd the use of this exemple: if his Imp. Majesty, to whom the welfare of his Subjects is justly dear, took so much care of their profit by the 17. Art. of the Treaty of Antwerp, as to prohibit the Subjects of the States from fishing in the sea near Blankenberg in the territories of the said States; how much more just is it for the States, to oppose this considerable navigation, undertaken at Ostend against the direct intention of so many Treaties, & from which we may very justly presage an irreparable loss not only to the Companies of the United Provinces, but also to the Republick it self?

FINIS.

APPENDIX N. I.

Ex. Em. de Meteren, de la Traduction Françoise, imprimée à la Haye *en* 1618. *Liv. XXII. fol.* 487.

L*E susdit* Goesman *avoit pareillement charge de se plaindre des Marchands d'Anvers, de ce qu'ils negotioient sous le nom des Hollandois ès Indes, & sous le nom des François & Ostrelins en Espagne, & se servoient ainsi de moyens & voyes obliques: car les Espagnols tachoient en toutes manieres de defendre ce trafic aux Provinces-Unies, pour ce qu'ils estimoient que par icelui ils trouvoient moyen d'entretenir la Guerre. Voila pourquoi aussi ils avoient défendu fort étroitement toutes les licences, & de ne laisser passer aucunes marchandises qu'on transportoit ou apportoit aux Provinces-Unies, & à cette fin fermérent le passage du Rhin par le moyen de Rhinberg: & l'Adelantado ou l'Admiral d'Espagne, prenoit tous les Marchands & Patrons, qui étoient en Espagne, prisonniers, & faisoit de grandes recherches & inquisitions, tant à visiter leurs Livres de comptes, qu'à les torturer, si tôt qu'il avoit decouvert le trafic qu'ils faisoient: puis après il condamnoit les uns aux Galeres, & les autres il les punissoit de mort. La recherche & l'examen qu'il faisoit, étoit de savoir, quel argent, & quels Reaux d'Espagne ils avoient (contre la defense faite) emporté hors d'Espagne, & si les Marchandises qu'ils avoient, ne venoient pas des Provinces-Unies, ou d'Angleterre. Voilà pourquoi aussi le susdit* Goesman *requit qu'on pût visiter les Comptoirs, Livres de Comptes, & écrits de quelques Marchands d'Anvers, pour voir si on ne trouveroit point telles ou semblables fraudes: car ils pensoient que par ce moyen ils ôteroient tout le trafic à leurs Ennemis; mais cela ne se peut pratiquer, ni en Anvers, ni ès Païs-bas. Tellement que le susdit Adelantado, après avoir exercé beaucoup de tyrannie à l'endroit des Marchands & Patrons du Païs bas en commun, il les contraignit enfin à s'accorder pour ce qui s'étoit passé, & leur fit payer, au mois de Mars l'an* 1601. *quelques six cent mille Ducats, ou davantage.*

No: II.

Edictum PP. DD. Ordin. Gen. Fœd. Belgii die 11. *August.* 1718.

D*E Staten Generaal der Vereenigde Nederlanden, alle dengenen die desen sullen sien of hooren lezen,* SALUT: *Doen te weten, also Wy onlangs goetgevonden hebben, het Octroy voor dezen aan de Oost-Indische Compagnie dezer landen verleent, en te meer-*

APPENDIX N°. I.

From the French translation of Emmanuel van Meterens History of the Low Countries, printed at the Hague in 1618. L. XXII. fol. 487.

THe said *Gusman* had also orders to complain of the Merchants of Antwerp because they traded to the Indies under the name of Hollanders, as they did also in Spain under the names of French or Easterlings, using thus indirect ways & methods: For the Spaniards tryed all ways to hinder the United Provinces from this trade, because they thought it furnished them with means of maintaining the war. 'Twas for this reason they had strictly forbid all Passports, & all exportation or importation of goods into the United Provinces, for which end they had lockt up the passage of the Rhin by the Fortresse of Rhinberg. In Spain the Governours or Admiral imprisoned all the Merchants or Masters of Ships, examined them & their books with great rigour, & even tortured them to discover what trade they were driving; & often condemned some to the Gallies & others to death. Their perquisitions tended to discover if any silver or Spanish Ryals were carried out of Spain, contrary to the prohibition, or if any of their goods were come from the United Provinces, or from England. So this *Gusman* required that the Counting houses, Books & papers of the Merchants of Antwerp might be examined, to see if there might not be found of these or such like frauds; for by those means they fancied they might cut off all the trade of their Enemys: but that was not practicable in Antwerp, nor in the Netherlands. Yet at last by the cruelties of the Governours, & the tyrannical usage of the Merchants & Masters of the Netherlands, they were forced to compound for what was past, & to pay in March 1601. some six hundred thousand ducats, or more.

No. II.

Edict of the H. M. Lords States General of the United Provinces, published on the 11 of August. 1698.

THe States General of the United Provinces, make known to all & every one that shall see or hear these presents, that we having thought fit lately to renew the Patent formerly granted to the East-India Company of these Provinces

meermalem gecontinueert, wederom te continueeren, ende te prolongeren voor den tyd van Veertigh Jaren, na Expiratie van het tegenwoordige Octroy, het welke eyndigt met dese loopende Eeuwe; en sulks tot op alle de Pointen ende Artykelen daar in, als mede in de Prolongatie van de twee-en twintigsten December sestien hondert twee-en twintig, ende in de ampliatie, en interpretatien van dien begreepen, mitsgaders op de Resolutien ende Authorisatien naderhand van tyd tot tyd daar op gevolgt, SOO IS 'T dat wy by dese Onse verkondinge en publicatie van de voorschreeven verleende Continuatie en prolongatie, aan alle en een ygelyk kennis hebben willen geven, en notificatie doen, *op dat een yder mogte weten, dat niemand anders als die van de gemelde Oost-Indische Compagnie geduurende den tyd van het voorschreeve Octroy, binnen de limiten van het zelve uyt deeze Landen zal mogen varen of handelen, en ten eynde alle pointen, vryheeden en voordeelen, aan de gemelde Compagnie geaccordeert, by alle en een ygelyk van de ingezetenen van den Staat onderhouden mogen worden, zonder daar tegen te doen directelyk ofte indirectelyk binnen of buyten 's Lands, op de pœnen in het selve Octroy begreepen. &c.*

N°. III.

Extract uyt het Register der Resolutien vande Ho. Mo. Heeren Staten Generael der Vereenigde Nederlanden.

Lunæ den 11 Augusti 1698.

De Heeren Gedeput: vande Provintie van Holland en Westvriesland, hebben ter vergaderinge voorgedraegen, dat, wanneer Haer Ho. Mo. Successivelyk hebben gelieven te prolongeren het Octroy aende Oost-Indische Compagnie deser Landen vergunt, deselve somwylen meede wel hadden gelieven van soodanige Prolongatien, by Placcaet alomme kennisse te geven, ten eynde alsoo een yder soude mogen weten, dat niemant anders, als die van de gem. Compagnie, geduurende den tyd van 't Octroy, binnen de limiten van 't selve, uit deese Landen soude mogen varen, ofte handelen, ende ten einden meede alle pointen vryheeden ende voordeelen aande gem. Compagnie geaccordeert, des te beeter by alle de onderdanen van den Staat onderhouden soude mogen werden, sonder daar tegen te doen, directelyk of indirectelyk, ende dat nogh binnen deese Landen, nogh daar buyten. Dat verders Haar Ho: Mo: tot maintien vande gem. Compagnie ende op dat deselve ook door geen indirecte wegen soude werden benadeelt, verscheyde Placcaten haden laten emaneren, en wanneer die of eenigzints in ongebruyk waren geraakt, ofte na de gelegentheyd van de tyd meer moesten werden geschikt, deselven Placcaten telkens hadden gerenoveert, specialyk meede die, waar door alle ende een yder wierde verboden vande eene zyde, eenige onderdanen, ofte

vinces, at different times continued, & now again to prolong it for forty years after th expiration of of the present Octroy, which ends with this century; & to confirmall points & articles therin contained, or in the Prolongation granted on the 22. Dec. 1622. or in the amplification or explanations of the same, as likewise in the Resolutions & Authorisations that have from time to timefollowed therupon. THEREFOR WE, by this Proclamation, give notice to all whom it may concern, of this new Prolongation abovementioned, that all men may know, that it is not lawfull for any other but those of the said East-India Company to trade or navigate from this Country, within the limits marked in the said Patent & during the term of years therin prescribed; and that all the Inhabitants of these Provinces may observe all the Articles, Libertys, & Privileges granted to the said Company, without doing any thing to the contrary, directly or indirectly, at home or abroad, upon the penaltys mentioned in the said Patent &c.

N°. III.

Extract from the Journal of the Resolutions of the H.M. Lords States General of the United Provinces, of Mundy 11 August 1698.

THE Deputys of the Province of Holland & Westfriesland have represented in the Assembly, that upon the several prolongations of the Patent of the East-India Company of these Provinces, their H. M. have commonly thought fit to give notice of such Prolongations by publick Proclamations affixed every where, that so every one might be warned that it was unlawful for any other but those of the said Company, during the term of years of the said Patent, to navigate or trade from these Provinces, within the limits there marked; & that all the articles, liberties, & privileges granted to the said Company might the better be observed by all the Subjects of this State, so as nothing might be done to the contrary directly or indirectly, either within these Provinces or abroad: And that their H. M. had made several Edicts for maintaining of the said Company, & for hindering its being prejudiced by indirect means, had frequently renewed them when they were any ways neglected, or when any conjuncture required it, & particularly that by which it is strictly enjoyned on the one hand that no body shall entice or engage any subject or inhabitant of this country especially seamen, to go to the East-Indies in any foreign service; all which & the pains enacted for the transgressors may be seen at length in the different Edicts of their H. M. of the 1 July & 9 September 1606. of the 8 December 1616. 14 December 1617. 4 of May 1632. 14 August 1674. & 8 October 1680. That the said States of Holland,

ofte inwoonders deeser Landen, en voornamentlyk eenige Zee-vaarende luyden te disponieren, ofte te huuren tot eenigen vreemden dienst na Oost-Indien; ende aan de andere zyde, zigh tot sodangen vreemden dienst te verhuuren, ofte te begeven, zoo als van alle het selve, ende van de peinen tegens de contraventeurs gestatueert, breeder konde blyken uit Haar Ho: Mo: successive placcaten van den 1 July en 9 September 1606. 8 December 1616. 14 December 1627. 4 Mey 1632. 14. Augustus 1674. en 8 October 1680. dat de Heeren Staten haare principalen op alle het geene voorz. aandagtelyk hebbende gereflecteert ende verders in achtinge genomen, dat het Octroy voor de gem. Compagnie onlangs wederom was geprolongeert, dienvolgende hadden geoordeelt, dat het van groote dienst ende vrugt zoude zyn, dat van deese laatste prolongatie meede by Placcaet van Haar Ho: Mo: alomme kennisse zoude werden gegeven, en met eenen gerenoveert specialyk den inhoude vande Placcaten hier boven gemeld, met die elucidatie van sodanige pointen, als sommige haar wel abusivelyk vermynen by de voor Placcaten niet te wesen verboden, hebbende vervolgens aan haar Heeren Gedeput: gelast, de saake te brengen ter kennisse van Haar Ho: Mo: en te versoeken, dat Haar Ho: by Placcaat nogmaals geliefden te ordonneren; Eerstelyk dat geen Ingesetenen, ofte Inwoonders deser Landen, souden vermogen geduurende den tyd van het voorn. geprolongeerde Octroy, dat is tot den jaare 1740 incluys, te varen of handelen op Oost-Indien, directelyk of indirectelyk, en selve meede niet te senden, ofte aan andere daar naar toegaande, 't zy beediende van de Compagnie ofte andere, meede te geven eenige goederen of coopmanschappen, op halve of meerdere of mindere winste, of ook eenige goederen of coopmanschappen van daar herwaarts te laten komen. Ten anderen dat geene Ingesetenen, of Inwoonders deser Landen, ende specialyk geen Zee varende luyden, haar zouden vermogen te begeven in dienst van eenige Koningen Princen, ofte buytenlandsche Oostyndische Compagnie, ofte ook wel van andere particuliere uytreeders, ofte handelaars in die Ryken, of Landen, om met derselver scheepen naar Oost-Indien te varen, ofte daar te handelen; ende by aldien zy zulx albereyts zouden mogen hebben gedaan, dat zy luyden de voorn. diensten zouden hebben te verlaten, ende hun ten langsten binnen den tyd van drie maanden weder hier te lande ter plaatse harer residentie te begeven. Ende ten derden, dat niemant van de onderdanen, ofte Ingesetenen van den Staat eenige inlaage zouden vermoogen te doen te participeren, ofte zigh in eeniger maniere te interfferen in eenige buyten landse Oostindische Compagnien ofte haar in te laten in eenige vaarten, of handel, dewelke door deesen, of geene particuliere uyt reeders of handelaars, uyt de voorn. andere Ryken of Landen naar Oost-Indien, zouden mogen werden ondernomen, ende dat op de peinen hier naar volgende: als namentlyk, ten opzigte van het voorz. verste lidt, op de peinen in het voorz. Octroy begreepen, ende daarenboven, dat het geene by de Contraventeurs inwogen voorz. naar Oost-Indien gesonden meede gegeven, of wel van daar ontfangen zoude worden, zoude moeten blyven ten behoeve van de gem. Compagnie, ende dat deselve Contraventeurs nogh boven dien zoude verbuuren viermaal soo veel, als het voorz. wer-

their Constituents, having seriously reflected on these maters, & considered that the Privilege of the said Company was lately prolonge'd again, were of opinion that it would be of good effect & use that this new prolongation were made publick every where by order of their H. M. & that at the same time the abovementioned Edicts were renewed, with certain explications of some points that several persons erroneously fancied were not comprehended in the Edicts they had consequently ordered their said Deputys to propose this to their H. M. & desire they would again statute by a new Edict; I. That no Subjects or Inhabitants of this Country shall be allowed, during the time of this prolongation, that is to the year 1740. inclusive, to navigate or trade to the East-Indies directly or indirectly, nor to send with any body going thither, either in the service of the Company or otherwise, any goods or merchandise, on half profit or more or less, nor yet to let any goods or merchandise be fetched from thence. II. That no Inhabitants of these Provinces, especially Seafaring men, shall presume to engage in the service of any King, Prince, or East India Company of another country, or of any other privat adventurer or trader in such Countrys, to sail or trade in their Ships to the East-Indies; or in case any should be so engaged that they shall immediatly leave such service, & return here again to their places of residence within three months at farthest. III. That no Inhabitant or Subject of this State shall take any share or portion, or be any way concerned in any forreign East-India Company, or in any way meddle in any navigation or trade that may be undertaken by any particular Trader or Adventurer of such foreign Countrys to the East-Indies: And that on the penaltys hereafter specified, *viz.* As to the first article that, beside the penaltys contained in the said Privilege, whatever shall be found so sent to the East-Indies by any person contrary to this prohibition, or received from thence, shall be confiscated to the profit of the said East-India Company, beside four times the value which such transgressors shall forfeit, to be applied one third to the discoverer, one third to the Officer that shall prosecute them, & the other third for the poor. As for the second Article, on the penaltys appointed against such delinquents by the forementioned Edict of 8 October 1680. And for the third Article, that the persons so transgressing shall forfeit the value of the summe or share they shall have engaged for or laid in in to such foreign E. India Company, or with such particular adventurers of other Countrys trading to the E. Indies, & that as often as they shall have laid in any summe, or engaged for any portion in such foreign Company or trade, or being once challenged for it shall afterwards continue in it, to be applied as a bove. WHERUPON after deliberation it is resolved and ordained that in conformity to what is here proposed a Proclamation shall be issued out, & be printed & published every where as soon as possible in the usual manner &c.

verbeurd zoude bedraegen, te appliceeren een derde voor den aanbrenger, een derde voor den Officier, die de Calange zal komen te doen, ende een derden voor den armen. Ten opzigte van 't voorz tweede lidt, op de peine van 't voorz laatste placcaat van den 8 October 1680 jegens de overtreeders van dien gestatueert. Ende ten opzigte van 't voorz derde lidt, dat de Contraventeurs des aangaande zouden verbeuren de waarde van de inlage, ofte van de portie, waar voor zy zullen hebben geparticipeert ofte wesen geintereſſeert in eenige buytenlandsche Oost Ind. Compagnie ofte in eenige vaarten ofte handel, dewelke door desen, of geene particuliere uytreeders of handelaars uyt andere Ryken ofte Landen, naar Oost-Indien zouden wesen ondernomen, soo meenigmaal zy de inlaage gedaan, ofte portie, ofte aandeel in de voorz buytenlandsche Compagnien vaarten ofte handel, genomen zullen hebben, ofte gecalangeert zynde, naderhand egter daarin mogten hebben gecontinueert; te appliceren als vooren. Waarop gedelibereert zynde, is goedgevonden en verstaan, dat conform het voorn. geproponeerde, een placcaat zal geemaneert, ende het selve ten spoedigste gedrukt en alomme afgesonden werden, om gepubliceert ende geaffigeert te werden naar behooren.

Accordeert met 't voorz Register.

F. FAGEL.

N. V.

Diploma Aug: Imp: Ferdinandi III. super art. 53. pacis Monasteriensis, die sexta Julii 1648.

Ferdinandus III. Divina favente Clementia electus Romanorum Imperator semper Augustus, ac Germaniæ, Hungariæ, Bohemiæ, Dalmatiæ, Croatiæ, Slavoniæ Rex, Archidux Austriæ, Dux Burgundiæ, Brabantiæ, Styriæ, Carinthiæ, Carniolæ, & Marchio Moraviæ, Dux Luxemburgiæ ac superioris & inferioris Silesiæ, Wirtembergæ, & Teckæ, Princeps Sueviæ, Comes Habsburgi, Tirolis, Ferreti, Kyburgi & Goritiæ, Landgravius Alsatiæ Marchio S. Rom. Imperii; Burgoviæ, ac superioris & inferioris Lusatiæ, Dominus Marchiæ, Slavoniæ, portus Naonis & Salinarum &c. Agnoscimus & notum facimus tenore præsentium universis, quod cum nobis ex parte Sereniſſimi Hispaniarum Regis Catholici & Consobrini, Generi & fratris nostri Chariſſimi, demiſſe fuerit expositum, in pace nuper inter Serenitatem suam ex una, atque Status & Ordines Generales Fœderatarum Belgii Provinciarum ex altera parte, Deo bene juvante, conclusa ac publicata, inter alia contineri articulum, Ordine quinquagesimum tertium, hujus qui sequitur, ex Gallico in Latinum translati tenoris.

Dictus

N°. IV.

Copie of a *Proclamation* published in JAMAICA against the Scotch Colony at Darien. Taken from the *Collection of State Tracts* in K. Williams Reign. Vol. III. p. 535.

By the Honourable Sir *William Beeston* Knight, Governour & Commander in Chief for his Majesty in the Island of Jamaica, and of the Territories & Dependencies of the same, & Admiral thereof.

WHereas I have receiv'd orders from his Majesty, by the Right Honourable *James Vernon*, one of the principal Secretaries of State, importing, that his Majesty was not inform'd of the intentions and designs of the Scots in peopling *Darien*, which is contrary to the peace between His Majesty and his Allies, commanding me not to afford them any Assistance: in compliance therewith, in His Majesty's name, and by his order, I do strictly charge and require all and every His Majesty's Subjects, that upon no pretence whatsoever they hold any correspondence with the Scots aforesaid, or give them any assistance, with Arms, Ammunition, provision, or any thing whatsoever, either by themselves or any other for them; nor assist them with any of their shipping, or of the English Nations, upon pain of his Majesty's displeasure, & suffering the severest punishment. Given under my hand & seal of Arms, the 9th. of April, 1699. and in the eleventh Year of the Reign of William the third, King of England, Scotland, France & Ireland, & Lord of Jamaica, Defender of the Faith, &c.

N°. V.

Act of approbation, given by His Imp. Maj. Ferdinand III. upon the 53. Article of the Treaty of Munster. July 6. 1648.

FERDINAND III. by the grace of God, elected Emperour of the Romans, ever August, & King of Germany, Hungary, Bohemia, Dalmatia, Croatia & Sclavonia, Archduke of Austria, Duke of Burgundy, Brabant, Stiria, Carinthia, Carniola, & Marquis of Moravia; Duke of Luxemburg & of the upper & lower Silesia, of Wirtemberg, & of Teck, Prince of Suabia, Count of Hapsburg, Tyrol, Ferret, Kyburg, & Gorlitz; Landgrave of Alsatia; Marquis of the holy Roman Empire, of Burgaw, & of upper & lower Lusatia, Lord of Marck, of Sclavonia, of Port Mahon & of Salins &c. We acknowlege & make

Dictus Dominus Rex obligat se effective ad procurationem continuationis & observationis Neutralitatis, amicitiæ & bonæ vicinitatis ex parte suæ Cæsareæ Majestatis & Imperii cum Dominis Ordinibus, ad quam continuationem & observationem prædicti Domini Ordines reciproce pariter se obligant, sequeturque super eo confirmatio suæ Cæsareæ Majestatis intra spatium duorum mensium, ex parte vero Imperii intra Annum a conclusione & ratificatione præsentis Tractatus.

Ac proinde supplicatum, ut Nos pro nostra parte dictum Articulum clementer approbare, ratum habere atque confirmare dignaremur. Nos, re mature ac diligenter deliberata, propropensissimo nostro in pacem quaqua versum promovendam ac propagandam studio, in ejusmodi petitionem clementer annuerimus, dictumque articulum ejusque contenta, quatenus ea ad Nos pertinent, pro nostra parte approbaverimus, ratificaverimus, prout hisce ex certa scientia, autoritate nostra Imperiali approbamus, ratificamus & confirmamus, eadem autoritate & scientia volentes, declarantes & statuentes, quod non modo nos contra eundem Articulum ejusque contenta, quatenus ea ad nos pertinent, directe vel indirecte nihil committere, sed nec ab aliis fieri vel committi permittere velimus: In cujus rei fidem præsentes manu nostra subscripsimus, & sigilli nostri Cæsarei appensione communiri fecimus: quæ dabantur in Arce nostra Lincii, Sexta Julii, Anno Domini 1658. *Regni Hungarici* 23 *Bohemici vero* 21.

FERDINANDUS.

Ferdinandus *Comes Curitus* V.

Ad mandatum S. Cæs. Majest. proprium

WALDERADE.

make known to all men by these presents that wheras it has been humbly represented to us in the name of the most serene Catholick King of Spain, our dear Brother, Cousin, & Son in law, that in the peace lately concluded, by God's grace, & published, between his Serenity on the one side, and the States General of the United Provinces of the Low Countries on the other, there is, among others, one Article, the fifty third in order, of the following tenor, as translated out of French.

The aforesaid King obliges himself to procure effectually the continuation & observance of the neutrality, friendship & good neighbourhood of His Imp. Majesty & the Empire with the said States; to which continuation & observance the said States also oblige themselves reciprocally: And this shall be confirmed by His said Imp. Majesty in two months, & by the Empire, in a year after the conclusion & ratification of this Treaty.

And being requested that we for our part would be graciously pleased to approve ratify & confirm the said Article, we having ripely & fully examined the matter, thro' our singular & earnest desire of promoting & maintaining peace every where, doe graciously grant this request, in approving & ratifying for our part the said Article & the contents therof in as far as they concern us; As we doe hereby, of our certain knowlege, & by our Imperial Authority approve, ratify & confirm them, willing, declaring & ordaining, by the same authority & knowlege, that nothing shall be done by us directly or indirectly against the contents of the said Article, as far as it concerns us, & likewise that we will not allow any thing contrary to be done or committed by others. In testimony wherof we have signed this with our own hand, & appointed our Imperial Seal to be annexed hereto. Given in our Palace of Lintz on the sixth day of July, in the year of our Lord 1648. & of our Reign in Hungury 23. in Bohemia 21.

Signed

FERDINANDUS.

Ferdinand Count Curtz Vt.

By express order of His Sac. Imp. Majesty.

WALDERADE.

www.ingramcontent.com/pod-product-compliance
Ingram Content Group UK Ltd.
Pitfield, Milton Keynes, MK11 3LW, UK
UKHW022128260726
13993UKWH00003B/1307

9 782329 263137